Work Well. Play More!

High Fives and Fist Bumps

This is one of the best books that I've read on how to create habits to live a more productive, clutter-free, and healthier life. If you're feeling overwhelmed, overworked, and tired, this book is a must-read! Marcey Rader provides a step-by-step guide to making the small to big changes that will transform your personal and business life.

— Sylvia Inks, founder of SMI Financial Coaching, LLC and author of Small Business Finance Book for the Busy Entrepreneur – Blueprint for Building a Solid, Profitable Business

I read a lot of business and self-improvement books; many sound the same and most lack ACTIONABLE steps I can take immediately. This book is different and fresh: you'll want to read it with your whiteboard clean and ready, because by the end of the book, you'll have a CLEAR plan for working well and playing more!

— Sara Shelp, VP Accounting | Business Operations, Spectra Logic

This book has given me real life, simple productivity hacks that I can implement now leading to a positive change in my business and personal life. I cannot wait to share this book with my family, friends, and employees. It's the best book I've read that gives a step by step plan to get better in your area of choice.

— Michael Clegg, Managing Partner, The Q Works Group

Marcey is a master at helping you make the change you need to get the life and results you want, whether you believe you can or not. Read this book and get started today!

— Eric Syfrett, Pastor and Financial Consultant

Change is hard. Even the changes I want for myself often seem unobtainable. Marcey Rader has broken the code and solved the daunting mystery of how to wade through our own proverbial muck and make change happen. Her easy to digest, step-by-step monthly guide gives me confidence that I can make it to the other side a healthier, happier and saner person who GSD!

— Lisa Wood, Sidecar Social Club

Marcey Rader's book will transform your life and help you become a happier and healthier you. Her steps for changes you can make to improve your health, declutter your mind and possessions, and increase your productivity without working longer hours are simple, easy to follow, and can be done over whatever timeframe you want. For me, it all started with Marcey's 25 in 25® program as a way to start incorporating more movement into my daily routine. I haven't looked back since!

— Mary-Lynn Fulton, Head of Clinical Trial Management, Vertex Pharmaceuticals

As a former journalist and PR professional, I consider myself well versed in the pillars of productivity to organize information and meet deadlines. As a part-time fitness instructor, I often counsel clients in the behaviors necessary to be at their best. I am also human, and I often don't practice what I preach. Especially when it comes to my personal life. This book reminded me that if I truly believe in the importance of my work, I need a responsible self-care plan.

Marcey Rader makes a compelling argument that productivity is directly related to overall health and wellness. She skillfully mixes practical, actionable advice and resources with relatable stories from her own life, proven methodologies and client testimonials.

Marcey practices what she preaches and I consider this to be a strong point of the book. She not only provides simple steps to change toxic behaviors that kill productivity but provides specific tools and steps to achieve a clutter-free, healthy, and productive life.

— Jessica Coscia, Coscia Communications

Also by Marcey Rader

Beyond Travel:
A Road Warrior's Survival Guide

Hack the Mobile Lifestyle:
6 Steps to Work Well and Play More!

Productive, Clutter-free, Healthy Living

One Step at a Time

Marcey Rader

Work Well. Play More!
Productive, Clutter-free, Healthy Living – One Step at a Time
Copyright © 2019 by Marcey Rader

www.marceyrader.com
www.workwellplaymore.com
www.workwellplaymore.com/books
www.workwellplaymore.com/masterclass

Printed in the United States of America
ISBN 978-0-9963763-2-7 softcover
ISBN 978-0-9963763-3-4 e-book

Book design by CSinclaire Write-Design

The publisher and author have strived to be as accurate and complete as possible in the creation of this book. Because technology changes and research evolves, some things suggested in this book may not be relevant at the time of purchase. All links in the ebook version are live as of October 2019 though, of course, there is no guarantee they will be live at the time you read this book. Because I change and I evolve, what I describe as my routine at the time of publishing, may not be my routine when you read this.

The information is based entirely on my own education and personal experience. However, I am neither a doctor nor a guru (nor even a tightrope walker), and this is not a substitute for hiring a doctor, so make sure you consult those smartie-pants before you even so much as implement one new behavior. What's included in the book are expressions of my opinion, so let it be known throughout the world, universe, and dark matter that I can't guarantee any outcomes, promise you'll lose 50 pounds, improve your productivity to reach Inbox Zero, or declutter your house until you only have 100 things. Follow the advice offered in this book at your own risk and free will.

While all attempts have been made to verify information provided for this publication, the publisher assumes no responsibility for errors, omissions, or contrary interpretation of the subject matter herein. Any perceived slights of specific persons, peoples, or organizations are unintended. Quotes and testimonials from my clients are with their permission because they are awesome. If you are reading this disclaimer, you are my people, and you are awesome as well.

This book is dedicated to my
Happiness Specialist/Customer Support/
Web Designer/Assistant, Rea Mae Donato.

You inspire me to be the best employer, boss, mentor,
and friend that I can be and to grow my company so we can
continue to help other women grow their companies through our
Kiva partnership. You are a unicorn in a world of mediocrity.

"The very best thing you can do for the whole world
is to make the most of yourself."
— *Wallace D. Wattles*

CONTENTS

FOREWORD

I am delighted to write this foreword not only because Marcey Rader is a powerhouse woman full of vivacious energy but also because I deeply believe in her teachings.

I first heard of Marcey's work when I invited her to speak at a women empowerment retreat I hosted. She led the group through a walking exercise that resulted in euphoria for all of the women in the room. To this day, I still remember the impact she had with her advice and incorporate her suggestion of "Walk + Talk" meetings, which has been a life game-changer.

Work Well. Play More! is a perfect guidebook for those who crave simplicity and space to live their most productive and healthy lives. As someone who has become a champion for self-care and minimalist living, her teachings resonate deeply with me. From my personal journey and work to empower women to access their best selves from skin to soul, I've seen firsthand how these intentional shifts can benefit your radiance, inside out.

The timing of this book could not be better. With tech

addiction and other distractions compromising our quality of life more than ever, Marcey's teachings are refreshingly easy to infuse into a busy lifestyle. Creating boundaries is a powerful first step to self-care, and from closet edits to desktop clean-ups, her process feels cathartic and healing.

You teach what you heal, and Marcey's journey from past to present is a beautiful testament to this belief. Her struggles with sugar, sleep, and staying healthy along with her resolve to rise above is now our gift of wisdom and learnings. She's even made it easy by creating bite-size prompts for the "novice, pro, and master" to do what you can for a more productive and healthy life.

I'm grateful to have *Work Well. Play More!* in my library of curated books, and I know you will be grateful too.

> *Here's to self-care, success, and savoring life,*
> *Angela Jia Kim*

Angela is the founder of Savor Beauty, natural skincare and spas inspired by Korean beauty rituals. As a recovering workaholic, daughter of Tiger parents, and former concert pianist-turned-beauty entrepreneur, she is a self-care advocate for busy women who do it all. Learn more at angelajiakim.com.

INTRODUCTION

It's no secret that there's a strong relationship between being healthy and being productive. Over the years, I've learned that engaging in just one unhealthy behavior can lead to a decrease in output in all areas of life. Of course, not being one to do anything halfway, my wake-up call came when I was diagnosed with three autoimmune diseases. I believed I was healthy, but I was traveling for work 48 weeks a year, training aggressively for triathlons and adventure races, sleeping from four to six hours each night, and was a total sugar addict. Yep. I broke myself. I had been firing on all cylinders and running on fumes. I was forced to take a step back and reassess. From this experience, I learned that health is the most valuable asset any of us has. Fortunately, I figured out how to put myself back together again using simple steps to become healthy, productive, and clutter-free. But let's back up and look at how I became broken.

Fake Healthy. Does This Sound Familiar?

I grew up in a Midwestern family that didn't eat vegetables (or at least anything that would pass for a *fresh* vegetable)

1

and sugar was a major food group. We pretty much lived on nachos, Hormel chili, bean burritos, bologna, ice cream, and chili pizza. When we did have a "vegetable," it was corn, potatoes, or canned green beans. I never had a pepper, mushroom, or anything green and leafy until I was in my twenties. (*Mom, I know that you are embarrassed when I talk and write about this, but it is real life, and I promise there are readers who grew up eating the same way.*)

My senior year of high school, when I was tired of being chubby, I embraced the new fat-free fad. If it had more than two grams of fat, it wouldn't touch my lips. I lost about 35 pounds, but my hair got thinner and my nail beds were blue. I remember one instance when I refused to buy a frozen yogurt because it was only 97 percent fat-free. I almost passed out on the hour drive home because I was so hungry.

This continued into college where my diet consisted of Snackwell cookies (raise your hand if you remember those!), unlimited frozen yogurt (you'll see that this becomes a staple) at the dorm cafeteria, pizza, and late-night trips to the Sunshine Café for biscuits and gravy (because hey, I was in college). I put ten pounds back on and started teaching aerobics to maintain some of my weight loss.

After college, I became a vegetarian, or in my case, a carbatarian because there still weren't very many veggies in my food repertoire. I subsisted on meat analogs (the vegetarian equivalent of processed bologna and hot dogs), bricks of tofu, bread, pasta, and (again) frozen yogurt. It wasn't until my early thirties that I really branched out and learned to cook, but because I traveled for business 45 to 48 weeks a year, I struggled to make cooking a regular habit.

I consumed processed, refined carbohydrates and sugars. I was a Frappuccino addict who fooled herself by thinking that because I got it "light" and without the whip, it was okay. I consumed artificial sweeteners like Crystal Light and Diet Mountain Dew because I believed that artificial sweeteners weren't harmful. (I mean what could be bad about zero calories, right?) After I learned how artificial sweeteners are one of the worst nutritional and political research conspiracies in history, I weaned myself off of those as well. **If there is one change I would tell someone to make in their diet immediately, it's to eliminate artificial sweeteners.**

But I continued to eat processed junk with ingredients I couldn't even pronounce until my mid-thirties. When I traveled, it was the worst. I consumed a steady diet of airport Auntie Anne's pretzels, frozen yogurt, Frappuccinos, and Clif Builder Bars. I started to compete in marathons and became a gel-sucking, sports drink-slurping runner, triathlete, and adventure racer who rewarded herself with a giant cookie the size of a small pancake from the bakery on Saturdays.

Looking back, I really can't believe I thought what I was doing was healthy. But hey, I was a vegetarian and a marathoner! I was well educated. I even had two degrees in Exercise Science. What I thought was healthy eating, however, wasn't healthy at all. When you eat a double-bacon cheeseburger, you know it isn't the best choice. Because I was eating frozen yogurt instead of ice cream or a soy burger instead of a hamburger, I thought I was doing the right thing. It wasn't out of ignorance because after earning my degrees, I studied nutrition with continuing education for my certifications. And I certainly wasn't alone in my misconceptions about what was healthy. Even the American Dietetic Association and the

USDA pushed artificial sweeteners back then. I, along with most other Americans, was duped into thinking that at least diet or light junk was better. As long as it wasn't high in fat, I reasoned, I was golden. Thankfully, knowledge and research about nutrition have grown by leaps and bounds in the last decade.

Perhaps the craziest thing of all is that even with all the artificial sweeteners, I still had a sugar addiction, which I came by honestly from my family. I would spend my days eating protein bars (25 grams), drinking mocha lattes (35 grams), and then get a cookie (31 grams) or brownie (30 grams) to take home and share with my husband—sugar, sugar, sugar. I had to have a sweet treat every night. I stayed at Doubletree Hotels when I traveled just because of the warm chocolate chip cookies.

As a consequence of my habits, I was always really fit but never really lean. Even training for Ironman Triathlons in my thirties, I didn't have the abs I have now in my mid-forties. I was never able to see definition until I changed my diet and cut out sugar and artificial sweeteners and added a serious amount of vegetables. **Abs are made in the kitchen.**

In January of 2014, six months after starting my business and four years and five doctors of trying to figure out unexplained symptoms, my world was rocked. I was diagnosed with Hashimoto's Autoimmune Disease, secondary Raynaud's Disease, and Pernicious Anemia, which changed my diet yet again. I tested positive for gluten intolerance and also discovered I had a sensitivity to soy. I spent about three months doing an autoimmune, Paleo, elimination, provocation diet, which was no easy feat. I may have even shed a tear the first week (okay, I cried like a big baby). But now I am proud to say I have a diet that really works for me, and I don't feel restricted at all. I got certified through the Institute of Integrative Nutrition and received two more nutrition certifications from the National Academy of Sports Medicine.

Currently, I eat a gluten-free diet and try to have as little soy as possible. (It's in everything!) I eat grass-fed beef, wild-caught fish, and hormone-free poultry. I max out at 1 or 2 servings of grains a day and eat at least 4 to 6 daily servings of vegetables (and corn and potatoes don't count).

Movement and Health

Exercise has always been part of my life but not always by choice. Growing up, I played group sports—volleyball, softball, basketball—and I ran track. I absolutely hated basketball, but living in Indiana, saying you hated basketball was like saying you hated kittens, so I played. I was chubby, so running track was hard and humiliating. I went to the second smallest school in the state where I once went an entire season without participating in one winning basketball game and only played in two winning volleyball games. Talk about a self-esteem booster! The rule in my house was that if I didn't play the sport of the season, I was essentially grounded for those months and couldn't have friends over or go to sporting or social events at school. So, I suffered through season after season and never played those sports again after high school.

All I wanted to do was dance. My senior year, when I got into the crazy fat-free phase, I bought my first exercise tape by Jody Watley. (Remember VHS? Remember Jody?) That tape changed my life. I did those workouts at five thirty almost every morning before school, even when my dad made fun of my dancing. (Note to all dads: do not do this to your low self-esteem, chubby teenager or any teenager for that matter.) This led me to become certified to teach aerobics in college, which progressed into running my first 5K my senior year.

Running 5Ks turned into 10Ks, which turned into running marathons, qualifying for Boston, and then switching to tri-athlons. After competing in two Ironman Triathlons during my heaviest year ever of travel, I switched to dirt sports. My obsession with triathlons was starting to go to my head. I began to quantify everything. I was up at four thirty on Saturday mornings, would ride my bike around my cul-de-sac to get the last 45 seconds in of my scheduled 6-hour ride, and didn't go out at night on the weekends to be fresh for my long run on Sundays. It was all too much, so I decided to try something different.

Dirt sports started with mountain biking, then ultra-endurance mountain biking, ultra trail running, and adventure racing. I loved the freedom and that my times didn't mean as much on the dirt. The result of a 7-minute mile on the road doesn't mean the same thing as the result of an 8-minute mile on a trail in the mountains over roots and rocks and running through streams. I also slowed down self-quantifying and participated in a 100-mile mountain bike race on a single speed bike with only my Timex watch—not even a bike com-puter. That was a significant mindset shift for me.

Adventure racing was fun and helped me move further away from the clock-watching and a perfect training regime life-style to one of flexibility, adaptation, and teamwork. I did over 30 adventure races from six to 30 hours and participated in the National Championships twice. Looking back, the stress of competing overnight in extreme temperatures did me no favors when it came to triggering my Hashimoto's and Raynaud's Diseases. What makes the body, breaks the body, and my aggressive racing and training schedule combined with the mental and emotional stress I was putting myself under at work broke me.

Hashimoto's Disease is a common autoimmune hypo-thyroid disease. I didn't cause it, yet I know I triggered it. This was my body's way of telling me enough is enough. It all imploded after one year when I was frequently traveling, racing a lot, and had more work stress than I thought possible. I was doing the job of four people for almost nine months and had incredible insomnia, managing on 4 or 5 hours of sleep a night (and a whole lot of adrenalin). For three years I saw different therapists and doctors and spent about $6,000 in copays and treatments to figure out what was wrong with me. I woke up with low blood sugar at three or four a.m., always felt super cold, would forget things, cried easily, and had significant digestive issues for almost four years. Because I identified with being healthy, no one—not even my closest friends—knew all of my symptoms. But the truth was I had made myself into a physical and psychological mess.

After my diagnosis, I went through the grieving process of no longer pretending I was the healthiest person in the room. I had started my coaching business six months earlier and thought, "How will anyone trust a health coach who isn't healthy?" I was also diagnosed with idiopathic hypothalamic hypogonadism (i.e., menopause caused by the hypothalamus). I had been in menopause since the age of 36, which has its own risks, and at the age of 40, I was put on hormones. I felt like an old woman.

With trepidation, I decided to write a "true confessions" article, and the response was overwhelming. I began to tell the truth about what was happening to me and received countless emails. Confessing, to my surprise, also helped me grow my coaching business. I started getting more and more clients with Hashimoto's and other autoimmune diseases. Finally, after seeing six different doctors, I found a program that kept me healthy while allowing me to move forward with my busy life. I took training in managing autoimmune diseases and now see the conditions as real gifts and manage my health well.

I ultimately retired from racing in September 2014. The thrill of competing no longer defined me as it had before, for which I am grateful. I have lived five lifetimes when it comes to racing and competing. A friend once asked me if I missed it because it was such a big part of my life. I realized that when I worked my corporate job, racing was an escape, and now that I had my own business, I didn't feel the need for it. My energy and passion had found a new outlet in helping my clients and growing my company.

Now, I train for life and longevity about an hour every day— lifting weights, running, mountain biking, practicing yoga, jumping rope, and dancing—and look for movement opportunities wherever I can. I do walking meetings; I hoop dance while I read; I use my FitBike sometimes when working; and I have a morning routine of meditation, gratitude, and heart rate variability tracking that keeps me sane. I feel and look better than I ever have before.

My nights of terrible sleep are much better, although I still have issues occasionally. I use self-hypnosis and meditation, a sleep mask, and Acoustic Sheep sleepphones to help me get my ZZZs.

Productivity

My struggles with productivity were mostly internal because I had inadvertently trained people that I was reactive. I didn't set appropriate boundaries, and I let other people control my agenda. I've always been fast at typing, reading, and "doing" whatever task I was performing, but I am very easily distracted and find that serious focus is still a behavior I have to practice. I would get anxious if I couldn't check my email often enough. I had so many email subscriptions and article feeds that I always felt behind. It all made me feel like I had much less time than I did because I had so much to read; it seemed like a part-time job. There were so many ways in which I was making more work for myself. I'm Type A (as in *Type Awesome!*), but that characteristic is rarely used as a compliment. My personality isn't going to change. But I've learned how to manage my Type A tendencies better. I still definitely Get Shit Done, only now I do it not because I work long hours but because systems are sexy, and I set them up to save myself from myself.

When I coach private clients, I can geek out all day on how to streamline email, tasks, calendars, and meetings. I love helping people find extra time that they swear they don't have. There's no "one-size fits all" when it comes to productivity. Mastering task management isn't the answer if the wrong boxes are being checked. People often go about their days being unnecessarily busy. I can tie and untie my shoes all day and be busy, but I'm not being effective. I often find with my clients that we have to look first at the tasks to figure out which ones will make them more effective and which ones really are just busy work. That's my line of genius: helping people stop the busyness and work on their businesses.

Clutter

I've never tried to keep up with the Joneses (where did anyone with the last name Jones get so much power anyway?), yet when I got into expensive sports like triathlons and adventure racing, the equipment started to take over my garage. At one point, I had four bikes (yep). I rode them all, but still, how many people need four bikes? I had books and CDs I didn't read or listen to and clothes I didn't wear. I lived in a house with a yard when both my husband and I abhor mowing. It caused friction between us and was never worth the energy of the argument.

I also had a lot of head trash. I pretended to do work on myself, but speed reading and then just going to the next chapter doesn't count.

I've worked with a few fantastic coaches in different areas where I know I need support. I believe everyone needs a coach or peer advisory group and not just because I am a coach, am in a mastermind, and am part of a Vistage peer advisory group. Coaches who don't have coaches are confusing to me. I'm never so full of ego that I don't think I have blind spots.

How did this book come about?

In 2009, I read *The Power of Less* by Leo Babauta, and my life path was forever altered. Babauta is adept at helping you break down any goal into manageable tasks. I decided to make small changes based on topics from the book. I started reading every minimalist and decluttering blog I could find—to the point of obsession. I knew I was changing—physically and mentally—and the methodical, planner side of me wanted to organize in an organized fashion. Also, since I had decided I wanted to make such an overhaul—a real transformation mentally, physically, and emotionally—I didn't want to set myself up to fail.

I decided on 100 things I wanted to change about myself and my surroundings and made a plan on a whiteboard. I decided to change one habit each in productivity, health, and physical/mental space. I worked on each habit for 4 to 8 weeks, depending on how hard it was for me to change and put a little check on my whiteboard every day that I did it. Now there are great apps that can help you keep track of habit changes but back then (in the Stone Age . . . I mean around 2009), there was just my whiteboard.

Even if you use an app, a notebook, or write in this book, I still recommend using a whiteboard too. Seeing that habit and those check marks every day in front of your face is inspiring and can hold you accountable. Once the streak starts, you don't want to stop it. I especially like whiteboard wall decals so you can peel them off the wall and move them, depending on what particular behavior you're working on (i.e., flossing your teeth every day is in the bathroom, but prepping your clothes at night before you go to sleep is in the bedroom) and you can replace them easily as you need to. I like to use **Post-it Dry Erase Whiteboard Film Surface** for my work.

Some of those 100 new habits were easy, like adding fruit daily, and others weren't, like checking email less often. I had my share of setbacks and restarted my streaks many times. But over the course of a couple years, I finally made it through all the habits on that whiteboard. I've included many of them in this book with a few adapted for technology and added some that are more recent behavior shifts.

Since the "whiteboard transformation," my husband and I have downsized one more time, completely paid off our house, and are debt free at 45 (me) and 50 (husband). We live in an 1,100 square-foot house and use the **KonMari** method regularly to keep from accumulating stuff. I have a stylist come to my house once a quarter to edit my closet. I keep it simple to reduce decision-fatigue.

I work with a coach who helps me avoid self-sabotage—as a recovering perfectionist and self-professed "prover" that I can do anything I put my mind to, I tend to go overboard with the *how* rather than focusing on the *why* when it comes to projects or sales. I'm part of a mastermind group of business owners, coaches, and speakers who challenge me and make me better onstage and off. I am in a Vistage peer advisory group that fills me up with what's possible in my business. I am in a 25-year relationship with my husband, Kevin, who has not only supported and accepted all the changes I have made but has made significant ones of his own.

Having lived through the experience of such a complete and wholesale life renovation, I wanted to share my story with you because I know how confusing behavior change can be. There are so many self-help books out on the market (I know! I've read most of them myself!), but while I have benefitted from parts of some of these books, I have also found many of them to be less than helpful for various reasons. Some are too abstract, academic, overwhelming, and (honestly) boring. Some do a marvelous job of helping you let go of baggage in one area of your life, but leave you hanging when it comes to making other changes. Many make unrealistic promises that require draconian rules no one with a life could ever possibly follow. When I wrote this book, I wanted to avoid all of these mistakes. **What I offer here is a step-by-step, practical guide to help you uncomplicate your life in three areas over time: productivity, clutter, and health.**

My clients are the ones who inspired me to write this book. I have the best job in the world—speaking on productivity and health behaviors, coaching people to live and work in their line of genius, and partnering with specialists who add so much value to what I do. I'm genuinely happier than I have ever been in my life, and I know it will only get better from here. You picked up this book because you feel a change a-comin', and you know it will only get better as well.

Habit change is hard. I believe in you. I do not take it lightly that you have decided to invest your money, time, and energy to commit to this book. I'm honored that you have chosen to bring me along on your journey.

High Fives and Fist Bumps!
Marcey

P.S. I hope you feel inspired by the quotes throughout this

book. These are from famous and not-so-famous people. Some are from attendees of my workshops and private clients who have mastered these habits themselves. I hope to receive many quotes from readers who have made a life change using their own whiteboards. Will you be one of them? Email me: habits @workwellplaymore.com

HOW TO USE THIS BOOK

This book is intended to be a guide for behavior change with clear goals and habits but without strict rules. Much like Tim Ferriss's *4-Hour Workweek* doesn't promise you will only have to work four hours and Erin Doland doesn't really expect you to literally *Unclutter Your Life in One Week*, I don't expect you to make all 100+ behavior changes in a year. You might, but that's not my intended goal for you. (However, if you want to make this *your* goal, go for it!)

This is not a "change everything all at once approach." Instead, I've broken down the possible changes into three levels of difficulty (Novice, Pro, and Master) and suggested one level of change in each of the three areas (productivity, declutter, and health) across 12 chapters. You could think of the chapters as corresponding to the months of the year or stretch out the time as long as you need to. You can choose the level you want to start with in each area and then once that habit (or habits) becomes like brushing your teeth, you're ready to choose the next set of behaviors you want to work on. You may not need to master a given level because it doesn't fit your lifestyle or be a goal that makes sense for you to achieve. A life example would be if you do not aspire to be a chef, you may only need to be able to fix a few simple meals to survive.

Here are a few action possibilities:

- You could choose a Novice, Pro, or Master step for each of the three areas (productivity, declutter, and health) to work on simultaneously, a step at a time.

- You could spend a year accomplishing all of the Novice steps in each of the 12 chapters, then go back and move onto the Pro habit changes for year two and go for the Master level after that.

- You could go through the Novice, Pro, and Master levels in one of the three areas (productivity, declutter, or health) before working on a different area. Want to just focus on decluttering? Great! Complete all of those steps before moving on to health or productivity.

This is what I mean when I say there are no hard and fast rules, and every habit change is a win. The only hard-and-fast suggestion I have is that you not do more than one behavior change at a time in one area, especially if you are embarking on one that is challenging or seems complicated. For example, don't try to do two health changes at a time, like increasing your vegetable intake and decreasing your sugar consumption. It's fine, however, to do work in more than one area—for instance, increasing your vegetable intake and decluttering the pantry. Hint: if it feels like too much to think about or change, you may be setting yourself up for failure. Often, we don't succeed because we are trying to transform too many behaviors at once. My suggestion is always to start with

Novice level unless the action doesn't apply to you. If it's easy, great! You get an easy win to propel you forward.

Approach this book as if you are ordering from a menu. Just as you select items from a menu, you can choose or not choose to change a particular behavior in a particular section. For example, you might not incorporate a recommended productivity habit because it doesn't make sense for your business or lifestyle. You might see a menu item as an opportunity to try the same dish you make at home but with a little twist of spice. It's entirely possible this book might inspire you to add a new flavor to one of your own habits!

If you have tried changing behaviors in the past and were disappointed because you didn't see the results you were hoping for, do not despair. The lack of results could have been for any number of reasons. Perhaps you decided to go from 0 to 60 (e.g., instead of gradually cutting back on sugar, you eliminated it completely, only to find yourself binging on cookies after a few days or a week and then feeling defeated). Maybe you fell prey to comparing yourself to someone else rather than focusing on your own progress (e.g., needing to be as organized as your sister, who happens to be a professional organizer). You might have tried to follow a cookie-cutter program when your life looks more like a layer cake (e.g., you quit the 12-Step Productivity Prowess Program on Step #1, and you're just not that into eating frogs).

Yet another reason previous attempts at change might not have worked for you is because you simply weren't ready to change. If you're looking for a book on the science behind habits, behavior change, and willpower, check out the Recommended Books section at the end of this book or in my hidden online bonus chapter at **https://www.workwellplaymore.com/books/ wwpm-bonus-sign-up/**. The one thing the science behind change makes clear is that before you can make any behavioral change stick, you have to be prepared and committed to doing what it takes to make the change. But it's also essential to realize real change takes time and often happens more slowly than we would prefer (damn that 21-day myth!). This is one reason I have set up the book the way I have with each chapter offering three levels (Novice, Pro, and Master) of habit change for each of the three categories (productivity, declutter, and health). This way, you can work more slowly or more quickly depending on where you are and what you need help with. You'll see a call-out at the end of each chapter—my print or digital version of a whiteboard—on the action step to take.

Take some time now to reflect on your past attempts at habit change. You could write about how you felt in those moments where things went off the rails for you, make a list of potential triggers that caused you to falter, and record what made you able to succeed in other cases, so you will know what to look for this time around and what steps to take to move toward success. Self-awareness is key.

In writing this book, I've tried to be mindful of potential setbacks. The restaurant is open. Here's your menu. Go ahead! Pick and choose, mix and match, and, above all, do what works for you. Why not start with the easy wins first?

How to know if you're ready to make a change

First, you made it this far in the book. Bravo! If someone gave you this book as a hint you didn't welcome, take a deep breath, get over yourself, and ask them to do it with you. While many people will begin this on New Year's Day because that's when people make resolutions, it can be started at any time of the year. There is something to be said for milestone dates like birthdays, back-to-school, new job, new home, baby, marriage, divorce, even Mondays. There are many milestones that can trigger behavioral shifts. Take advantage of them!

On the other hand, you may have picked up this book because you have been through a significant life or work transition recently (e.g., marriage, divorce, getting a new job, or a promotion) and suddenly feel out of alignment or out of your depth. Perhaps you've been living with pain or feeling "not quite yourself" for months or years. Or maybe you recently received some less than good health news from your doctor. Whatever the reason, you are ready to show up for yourself now, and that's awesome!

My big life triggers for behavior change throughout the years were:

- Moving
- New job
- A rough year with my husband about 13 years ago—I won't pretend that business travel didn't put a dent in my marriage, but it taught me boundaries, and we came out better on the other side.
- Desire to be debt-free
- Starting my business
- Diagnosis of multiple health issues

Do you see yourself in any of these?

Whatever your desire, you have to be ready. Doing it because you're trying to impress or keep up with someone else isn't going to propel you. Think inspiration (a pull) instead of motivation (a push). What is inspiring you to change?

Some psychologists look at the Transtheoretical Model of Stages of Change to help determine whether a patient is ready to make a change. This model divides behavior change into six categories[1]:

1. **Precontemplation** – Not ready to make a change in the next six months. Underestimates the positive benefits and overestimates the consequences of changing behavior. If this sounds like you, put down the book and come back to it in six months or gift it to someone.

2. **Contemplation** – Intention to start within six months but still not entirely on board. If this sounds like you, read the book and set a future plan to start with a natural behavior change that will be a quick win or highlight all the ones you already do and high-five yourself!

3. **Preparation** – Ready to make a change in the next 30 days. You've set the date you're starting, and you have your first few habits to work on written on the whiteboard.

4. **Action** – You're doing it!

5. **Maintenance** – You've been doing it for more than six months and intend to keep it up. You can use this book to stay inspired and keep fine tuning your habits.

6. **Termination** – Fully ingrained, no desire to revert back

to past behaviors, and you are cruising. It's a brush-your-teeth habit, as in you would never go a day without brushing your teeth, right? (If not right, please don't share this with me—ick!) If this is you, please buy this book for everyone you know and rave about it in an online review!

Here are just a few more tips before we get to the nitty gritty:

- As you go through each chapter, write down your *why*— *why* do you want to do this change? Then write your plan, any triggers, obstacles, replacement habits, and how you will get support.

- Use a whiteboard or an app like **Coach.Me** so you can see your streak. I like my whiteboard decals from Amazon so I can make my board as big as I want and place it wherever I want without messing up my wall. My preferred brand is **Post-It Dry Erase Film Surface**.

- Enlist support. Tell people what you are doing. Ask for accountability from someone you won't resent holding you to your goals. (My husband does not like for me to be his accountability partner. You may feel the same about someone in your life.) Use a website like **www.stickk. com** and pledge to an anti-charity if you think it will be a real struggle for you. If you want to learn how my client Helen used stickk, visit **https://www.marceyrader.com/ how-helen-moses-stuck-to-her-goal-with-stickk/**

- Join my membership program where I host webinars for the corresponding habits each month and you'll have a community of people working on the same habits you are. **www.workwellplaymore.com/masterclass**

- Have a plan for your saboteurs. Whether it's a person, place, event, or thing that could potentially derail you, map out your plan ahead of time for how you will handle it. You will have saboteurs. You will have setbacks. I had plenty, but I didn't let it stop me. I didn't wait until the next day or the following Monday to start. I began right then, at that moment, and even that was a behavior shift.

- Keep in mind that the first few days of any change are the hardest. You are fighting existing behaviors or paradigms that have been with you for years. At some point, you'll turn a corner, and it will start to get easier. Then you'll get met with a saboteur (see above). That's why it's important to plan ahead for those.

- Refer to yourself as how you want to be. If you don't currently exercise, refer to yourself as an exerciser. If you are a procrastinator, say that you are a person who Gets Shit Done (on time!). If you come home to an empty fridge after work, you are now a person who plans and preps meals ahead.

- Have a reward in mind! Every time you successfully complete a habit, make sure to reward yourself. Writing a list of all the things that make you feel happy, abundant, pretty, sexy, smart—whatever it is—can help you with your reward list. I like having my car really clean so getting my car detailed is a great reward for me. Just make sure the reward isn't always an ice cream sundae! :)

- Want an easy way to get to all the resources provided throughout the book? Sign up for the online bonus chapter at **https://www.workwellplaymore.com/books/**

wwpm-bonus-sign-up/ to get loads of discounts, extra training and direct links to everything you need.

REFERENCES IN THIS CHAPTER

[1] http://sphweb.bumc.bu.edu/otlt/MPH-Modules/SB/
BehavioralChangeTheories/BehavioralChangeTheories6.html

MONTH ONE

PRODUCTIVITY:
Notification Distractions

Notifications alert you to the fact that you have a message somewhere. Your smartphone may ring, buzz, or give you a visual cue (or all three) to let you know you have a voicemail, an email, a social media message, an app update, or whatever. These notifications are distractions. Being more productive calls for reducing such distractions. Let's focus on tips for doing that here.

Novice: Notification Elimination

Captive (noun): A person who has been taken prisoner or an animal that has been confined. Merriam-Webster

Do you ever feel like your mind is chasing squirrels? Are you constantly distracted by all the rings, pings, buzzes, and knocks? Do you feel like your smartphone holds you captive? Turning off your notifications can put you back in control

25

of your technology and allows you to get things done faster and more effectively because you aren't losing focus each time a notification pops up on one of your devices.

When we get interrupted, it causes stress, frustration, and increased time pressure.[1] If we pause what we're doing to address the interruption, we risk getting pulled in a totally different direction. Even if we get back to the original task relatively quickly, we have to refocus on where we left off, and we may feel the need to work faster to compensate for the lost time. The pressure and need to increase speed can sometimes result in making mistakes.

- According to digital distraction researcher Gloria Mark at the University of California, Irvine, it takes an average of 25 minutes (!) for the focus to return to the original task after an interruption.

- According to an Asurion study, Americans check their phones an average of about 80 times per day or once every 12 minutes *while on vacation*.[2] With tracking now available in smartphones, we can monitor our own pick-ups and usage.

The very first thing I do with my private clients when we are working on email is to disable any pop-up or banner notifications on their phones and computers that aren't necessary to them. Email is a necessity, but for most people, reacting as soon as an email comes in is not the best use of their time.

Notifications create reactivity instead of responsiveness. To effectively respond to emails and other work requests, we need to prioritize, and that means looking at a list of tasks with a cool head so we can focus on what needs to be done when. When we are continually being alerted to this and that and who and what, we never have time to focus. Each request feels urgent, so we react with urgency. Then, what's worse, we teach people that we are reactors and it becomes an expectation. Suddenly, we are living by their timelines and rules rather than our own.

A response is defined as timely within your boundaries and not done out of a false sense of urgency or telepressure. I respond to emails, texts, and voicemail in a timely manner, but I am not reactive and do not respond immediately when it's not warranted.

Note: If your job requires reactivity, (e.g., you're in customer service), this may be an item on the behavior menu that you have an allergy to, but you could turn off other notifications, like social media, that do not require your reactive attention.

Also, if you think you can tune out notifications, you're wrong. It affects everyone to varying degrees. People will often tell me, "When I get a notification, I just ignore it." Well, the very fact that you knew you got one means that you didn't actually ignore it. Notifications trigger the involuntary part of your brain. You can't help it. They also elicit a dopamine response, which is the same one you get from gambling and other potentially addictive behaviors.

Here's how to turn off notifications:

In Outlook
- Select the **File** menu and choose **Options**

- In the left area that lists the various categories, choose **Mail**
- In the **Message Arrival** section beneath **When new items arrive in my inbox,** uncheck all the checkboxes (no sounds, no notifications, no alerts!)
- Close out of all of these windows

In Gmail
- Go to **Settings**
- Look under **General**
- **Notifications** - **Mail Notifications**: "Off"

> *I will turn off all unnecessary notifications (sounds, vibrations, banners, and pop-ups) on my computer and phone.*

Pro: Badges

Badges are the little numbers on your phone or application to let you know that you have a new message, push notification, voicemail, or invitation. For most people, this number calls to them until they open up the application to see what's there. Our Fear of Missing Out (FOMO) makes us curious to see if it's essential. For the most part, badges are an unnecessary distraction and only the most critical badges should be turned on.

Unless you are a social media marketer, there is no reason to have social media badges turned on in your phone or tablet. Knowing immediately someone liked your post or photo isn't urgent. The rule of thumb is if you are going to go into that application at some point that day or in a timely manner, whatever that means depending on the application, keep those badges off. You don't need them. The only badges I have on my phone are text and voicemail because I see those as more urgent. I also have Voxer badges on because that's how I communicate with my private clients, but that app is on the second swipe screen of my phone and I have to be intentional to see it by swiping.

No, you don't need to see that you have ten unread emails. It doesn't matter if you are going to go into your email at some point (and I'm betting you won't go more than a day without checking email, even while on vacation). Take those badges off too!

Here's how to turn off badges:

iPhone
- Tap the **Settings** icon on the iPhone's home screen and then tap **Notifications**
- Scroll down the Notification Section and select the apps you want disabled from using badge alerts
- Tap the **Badge App Icon** button to toggle it from "On" to "Off"

Android
- Open the **Settings** app and go to **Apps** & **Notifications**
- Tap **Notifications**
- **Disable** app icon badges by flipping the **Allow icon badges** or dots to "Off"

> *I will turn off all non-essential badges on my phone.*

Master: Do Not Disturb

We all need focus time and Do Not Disturb (DND) blocks can help us do this. My phone is in "Do Not Disturb" mode almost all day long because I'm either working and want to concentrate, with a private client, or speaking. Fortunately, in my business, most people set up an appointment before calling me and don't just ring me out of the blue, but if they do call, they can always leave me a voicemail. Having DND on also keeps me from getting interrupted by telemarketers or robocalls.

If you have a business or job where you need to have your phone on, think about a time of day where you need to have focus or quiet and turn on DND for even just 30 to 60 minutes. Create boundaries for your morning or evening time when you want to focus on yourself or your family. I have an automatic DND on my phone from eight p.m. to nine a.m. This means that my phone goes into that mode and only calls or texts from people on my "Favorites" list, which currently is only immediate family, get through to me. I have to intentionally look at my phone if I want to see a text or voicemail. In the morning, it means I'm not interrupted during my most productive time, during a workout, or while meditating. My friends know if they text me in the morning, it won't wake me up or bother me because my phone is in DND. I'll look at it when I'm ready.

Can you create some white space and quiet time where your phone is on DND? What about during dinner, Netflix with the family, or while you work out? It doesn't just have to be at work.

> **I will create Do Not Disturb time during _____.**

DECLUTTER: Digital Files

If the term "declutter" brings to mind organizing and cleaning out physical spaces, that's reasonable. I'll share lots of tips for decluttering physical spaces in what follows. In this section, though, we'll focus on decluttering our digital lives. We'll start with your computer.

Novice: Clean Your Desktop

Did you think I meant your physical desktop? Nope. I want you to declutter your electronic desktop. First, all those files on there are slowing down your computer speed. Second, half of them are outdated, irrelevant, and keeping you from feeling at ease.

A few years ago I had a client who had a desktop background of a photo of her and her infant son at the beach. I could hardly see the picture because of all the files she had on her desktop. When I started asking her about the documents, she didn't know what some of them were and had to open them to know.

"Don't you want to see that little baby belly?" I asked her.

That became her goal: to reduce the number of files until she could actually see that cute little guy and feel joy instead of overwhelm when she opened up her computer. Your child, family, or vacation photo should never be the backdrop for files that make you feel overloaded.

I have three recommendations for wallpaper on your desktop.

Choose the one that speaks to you:

- Make a list of your top three priorities or goals for the month or week and make it your wallpaper (bonus productivity booster!)

- Choose an inspiring photo that makes you happy

- Choose completely white wallpaper to remind yourself to create more white space in your life

I do have one folder labeled "Temporary" that I keep on my desktop and purge monthly, and typically my wallpaper is a vacation photo to represent Playing More!

> *I will remove the files from my desktop and create a backdrop that makes me feel joy, at ease, or is a reminder of what I want to achieve.*

Pro: *App Removal*

How many apps are on your phone that you don't use?

In 2017, the average user had about 90 apps on their phone and used about 35 per month.[3]

Unused apps are sucking up your storage. Why make your eyeballs do the work and scan over that junk every time you look at your phone? Apps are so fast to download, many can be Just in Time (JIT) such as airline or hotel apps if you don't travel frequently or shopping apps if you only go to the store a few times a year.

Removing apps can also be helpful to curb impulse shopping (the Amazon Prime app can bankrupt you), to spend less time on social media, or to decrease your gaming. These three types of apps are often used out of boredom. There might be other things you could do in those moments instead—like practicing a breathing technique while waiting in line or just thinking while going up in the elevator for 12 seconds. Yes, you can actually just "thinkitate" sometimes and do nothing. We did it all the time before we had smartphones attached to our hands.

Here's how to offload some of those 55-ish apps you don't use:

Android devices
- Open the **Google Play Store app**
- Go to the **menu** in the top-left corner of the screen
- Sort by **Last Used**
- **Select** the apps you wish to uninstall

Apple devices
To offload apps, which takes the app off of your device but continues to store the data in the cloud if you want to reinstall one of them later.
- In **Settings**, go to **iTunes** and **App Store**
- Scroll to **Offload Unused Apps** and toggle "On"

To delete apps
- Go to **Settings**
- Tap **General**, then **iPhone Storage**—all your apps will be listed here with the largest at the top
- **Delete!**

> *I will delete all apps unused within the last _____ months. I will delete _____ (choose a gaming, social media, or shopping app that gives you regrets or you tap out of boredom). Instead of going to _____ app out of boredom, I will _____.*

Example: I will delete all apps unused within the last three months. I will remove Amazon Prime and force myself to visit the website intentionally on my computer or through the browser. Instead of going to LinkedIn out of boredom, while waiting in line, I will think about relaxing my shoulders and take deep belly breaths.

Master: Contact Purge

How many friends can you really have? Who *is* Janet Bakersmith?

I'm proudly LinkedIn only, but even when I had Facebook for personal use, I only had 20 friends, on purpose, because I only wanted to see the feeds of my real friends or people I cared about. I didn't want to waste time seeing people that I knew 20 years ago or people I probably would never see again. In January 2019, I quit Facebook and Twitter and went to LinkedIn only for my business. I have no personal social media accounts and have never felt happier. Fear of Missing Out? Nada.

This one may be extreme for some of you (hey, that's why it's a "Master" behavior change) and for some businesses, it could even be the death of them, so they should not do it. For me,

I'm able to have a thriving business and personal life without social media accounts. This also allows me to go on vacation and take a photo for *myself* without thinking about posting it for everyone else to see. Are the photos you take for your memories or to show other people what you are doing? Since this habit isn't for everyone, let's talk a little about minimizing our circle of "friends and influencers" and focus on what and who matters.

To baby step it, you could start with your phone. Go through your list of contacts one letter a day, deleting all the names that you have no idea who they are or who you won't need to contact again (e.g., you don't need to store the phone number of your ex-landlord from three years ago). This could be an easy waiting room task. It feels good to scroll down my list and only see people I know.

On Facebook, you can always just hide people, so you don't see their feeds. But why not just unfriend them? Because the language is too harsh? Well, isn't calling someone you met at a festival for five minutes a friend a little extreme also?

Back to the hiding . . . this is good for your aunt who posts political propaganda or your co-worker down the hall who might get offended and make things a little awkward for you IRL (in real life), but most people don't even notice when you unfriend them. Here's how I did my first purge when I mistakenly started friending and following everyone back in the day. The full size decision tree is available in the online bonus chapter, but you can get the idea of the flow here:

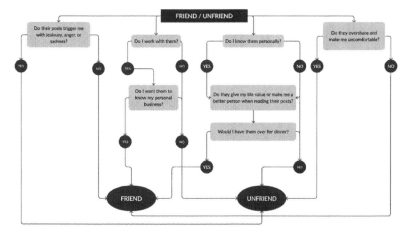

Those were my first easy run-throughs of my list. If you have a business, I would not suggest you start unfriending or unfollowing people or companies. Start with your personal feed first.

> *I will remove people or businesses that do not meet the following criteria* _____ *so that I am able to see the feeds of the people or businesses I actually care about.*

HEALTH: Portion Control

Twenty years ago, 6.5 ounces was considered a serving of soda. A bottle of Coke was sold to serve three people. Now a 20-ounce per person serving is the norm and people walk around with 36 or 48 ounce Yeti buckets (and drink more than one throughout their day!). Serving sizes are tricky and unrealistic. Most people are not going to buy a bottle of their favorite beverage and share it or save some of it for later. When they open up that pint of ice cream, they aren't going to split it four ways or eat it four different times. We're used to those oversized restaurant-sized portions so common today. My philosophy is if a restaurant has to serve quantity, it's because they can't serve quality. How can you trick yourself in this super-sized world and overcome portion distortion?

Novice: Hide and Seek

Brian Wansink (*Mindless Eating: Why We Eat More Than We Think*, New York: BantamDell Books, 2006) talks about the "mindless margin," between 50 and 300 calories, which is the range we tend to overeat if we're not consciously aware. This happens more when snack food is convenient, because we eat it subconsciously.

This mindless margin can add up to 10 to 30 pounds a year!

Just seeing food can trigger the release of dopamine in your brain and start a craving. Every time you see something to eat, your mind has to decide whether to eat it or not. This can cause you to have decision-fatigue, and your desire wins the battle. The office candy jar can be the death of a healthy meal plan to some people who can't take the smell or proximity. Wansink, who is the director of Cornell's Food and Brand Lab, found that people who sat within a six-foot radius of a dish of Hershey's Kisses ate on average nine pieces a day compared to four or five per day for those outside of this area. When the dish was opaque, everyone ate two fewer on average.

The lesson? Put food like cookies, chips, and candy that you don't want to eat as much of in opaque containers and the food like fruit, veggies, and nuts that you do want to eat in clear containers. Go even further, like I do, and freeze the extra treats and put them inside an empty vegetable bag or box. You can also put treats in a cabinet that requires a stool to access or, like I do, in a deep freezer located outside of the kitchen.

> *I will put all of my treats that I want to eat less of in opaque containers and in hard-to-reach places. I will choose to sit or stand as far from the candy bowl or treats as I can at the office or at parties.*

Pro: Right-Size It

Eat from small plates and bowls when you can. Restaurant dishes are the size of serving platters at home. This is not normal! Just like having more time means we will fill that time with things to do, having a bigger plate or bowl makes us feel like we need to fill the space. Use smaller size plates and bowls at home to trick the brain into thinking the portion of food is bigger.

The opposite is true when it comes to beverages. A beverage in a taller glass looks like more to the eye. I used to pour our Kombucha tea into a tumbler. When I poured the same amount into a tall glass, my husband thought it was too much and couldn't drink it all. But it was simply a trick of the eye. When people drink alcohol out of a short glass, they tend to drink 20 to 30 percent more than they do when they use a tall glass. The exception to this rule is drinking wine out of a wine glass. If you have huge wine glasses, you're more likely to serve bigger pours to fill the space. Is that wine glass you're drinking out of really a bowl? Also, because we don't typically fill up wine glasses, it can be hard to judge how much you've had at the end of a meal. Always beware when someone offers to "top you off" before you've reached the bottom of your glass. That's a recipe for drinking more than you intend. I once gave my friend a wine glass with two lines on it. One line for "Merlittle" and the other for "Merlot."

I eat off of smaller bowls and plates whenever I can. I use chopsticks and demitasse spoons for most meals at home and even travel with Titaner titanium chopsticks. Not only does using chopsticks force me to eat slower and take smaller bites but it also makes me feel fancy.

> *I will choose smaller plates and utensils when serving myself food.*

Master: *Containerize It*

This step is Master level because it requires more work and planning. The next time you make or buy treats that you want to eat less of, portion them out into individual baggies or containers *as soon as you get them*. I do this with any desserts or cookies and put them in the freezer. They can last for months this way. I also containerize (yes, I made the act of putting food into a container a verb) veggies that I want to take with me for the week to make it easier to grab and go.

> *I will separate _____ into reusable containers or bags as soon as I get them to avoid the temptation of eating more than I want to.*

REFERENCES IN THIS CHAPTER

[1] https://www.ics.uci.edu/~gmark/chi08-mark.pdf

[2] https://www.asurion.com/about/press-releases/
americans-dont-want-to-unplug-from-phones-while-on-vacation-
despite-latest-digital-detox-trend/

[3] https://www.appannie.com/en/insights/market-data/
apps-used-2017/

PRODUCTIVITY:
Folders and Filters

One of the beautiful things about technology is how it makes us more productive. Of course we all know technology also gives us an additional excuse to be less productive (hello, Pinterest rabbit hole). But if we actually use the tools technology offers us to make ourselves more productive, we can discover a whole world of possibilities. When we're mindful about the folders we create (both electronic and paper) and the filters we use, we can be more efficient. Let's look at behavior changes related to folders and filters.

Novice: Streamline Folders and Labels

Do you have so many folders in your inbox, you don't even know what's in them and you have to peek inside to see what's stored there? Do you have duplicate folders because there are so many you don't even realize you already have one? Stop hyper-organizing. This actually makes it more challenging to search.

Note: In older versions of Outlook, you are searching in a folder. In Gmail or G+, it is a label. A file can have multiple labels. Consider it more like a sticky note.

With most current email systems, the search capability is so extraordinary that if you archive a file, it's super quick to search for it. I only have a few folders/labels because I use my search function. My labels are part of my client relationship management (CRM) system and include Prospects/ Clients, Speaking, Networking, and Opt-Ins. If I'm looking for an email, I type the subject and the person who sent it and any emails related to that search criteria pop up. By using the search feature, you have just removed the act of determining which is the correct folder for the email (Does the receipt from your annual renewal for Acme Organization go in Receipts or Acme?), dragging it to a folder, and then searching within that folder. If you must have multiple folders or labels, a good rule of thumb is never have more labels than you can see without scrolling and always know what is in each folder. When I ask a client what they use X folder for, many clients have to open it to see. If there is any scrolling involved or if it takes more than one click, you are hyper-organizing.

Is your motto "a place for everything and everything in its place?" This hyper-organization in your inbox can be a form of procrastination. I've had clients with 20 to 30 folders or labels and only two or three emails in more than half the folders. This causes them to scroll to find or drag to the folder. It's a waste of time and leads to decision fatigue. So what happens? They just leave them in their inbox, which can work for some people, but I like to see only what is current and relevant in front of me. Not old emails.

Have as few folders as possible and trust your search function. If you have fewer than ten emails or five documents on a subject, you don't need to create yet another folder for it. And please, don't create sub-folders—that creates a double-click to get to them!

Here's how to streamline your email folders and labels:

In Outlook
- **Archive** all the old folders you never use by dragging them to the bottom of your list
- Consider putting them into one folder called "Archives" or "Old Folders"

In Gmail
- Get rid of any labels you aren't using within your **Settings—Labels**
- Scroll to the bottom and remove or hide

I'm not recommending having zero folders or labels, but do have the minimum that you can. Use the search function!

> *I will streamline my folders and labels by archiving or deleting unnecessary ones. I will know what is in the folders and labels I use. I will try to be scroll-less, only having as many folders or labels as I can see without scrolling.*

Pro: *Create Rules and Filters*

Note: In Outlook, it is a rule. In Gmail, it is a filter. I will refer to it throughout as a "filter."

I apply filters that tell my email program if a message arrives from a specific email address, it automatically gets sent to a particular label before or after I open it, depending on the filtering rule. This saves me a step. Instead of opening and dragging an email or even opening it at all, the email automatically goes into a folder (or label) where I can choose to view it later. I do this most often with emails I don't need to read or those that are more of an FYI. Remember, if you do this and later realize you need to read the email, you can always use the search bar or simply open the label and find the email.

Creating rules in Outlook works the same way as filtering in Gmail. By merely filtering an email to bypass my inbox, it saves me from having to delete or archive when I don't need to look at it. I may want access to an email later but not need to see it every time I open my email program. This is why filtering is effective. Emails can go automatically to archive or to a specific label.

> *I can't tell you what a difference the labels make–especially the red John label for the emails from my son's school. I haven't missed any action items since!* — **Barbara I.**

Do your family members forward you emails that don't align with your values, and you don't want to read them, yet you can't unsubscribe? Create a filter. If an email comes from *AuntSally@yahoo.com* and has *"FW:"* in the subject line, it automatically skips my inbox and goes straight to archives.

This works great for relatives who send me political, religious, or sensationalized emails without checking the source before hitting the send button. This is called Internet gossip. Don't do it. If Aunt Sally sends me a message that doesn't have "FW:" in the subject line, it comes to my inbox.

Items you could filter include:

- Automatic responses or notifications

- Receipts from online purchases – One of my clients is an interior designer, and the number of receipts and invoices she gets is incredible. To be able to find them quickly, I created a filter for anything that says "Invoice," "Statement," or "Receipt" in the subject to be labeled and filtered out of the inbox. She can see when something new comes in straight to that label and can find it easily without searching through her inbox. It also doesn't distract her from important emails because most of the receipts she doesn't even need to see.

- Statements from your bank that you can review within your online account

- Bills that you have set up for auto-pay

- Mass emails from people who send from their personal accounts and you can't get off their list – Since there is no way to unsubscribe, you have to filter these out.

- Employee emails that don't pertain to you – You don't need the company kickball information when you work remotely and aren't on the kickball team.

To uber-filter, sign up for **Unroll.Me**. Unroll.Me rolls up all your newsletters, digests, and notifications into one simple email delivered morning, afternoon, or evening. You can determine which emails you want to be rolled up and which ones you want to stay in your inbox. It also allows you to unsubscribe in one click. It's the number one program I recommend to my clients. The only thing that bothers me about it is that it has advertisements within the digest. I'd gladly pay for it to remove the ads. Unfortunately, this is not an option, and Rakuten Intelligence, who owns Unroll.Me, says the ads allow it to continue offering the service for free.

Another important item to note: you are not actually unsubscribing; you are sending them into an Internet black hole. This means the person you are unsubscribing from gets no notification that you did it (great if that newsletter is coming from someone who will get offended if you want to stop hearing from them). You also can add newsletters you have unsubscribed from back in your inbox or roll-up if you change your mind. You can do this without having to visit that specific website. On the flip side, for business owners who send newsletters, you won't see that someone has unsubscribed, and this does skew your numbers and make it look like you have more readers than you do.

Another excellent program is **Sanebox**, which can help filter out unwanted newsletters and send them to a "black hole" so you don't have to decide to read, delete, or unsubscribe.

To create a filter in Gmail
- With the email open, click on *More* in the top right corner
- **Filter Messages Like These**

- Enter the *From* and any other information that is critical i.e. *Subject*
- *Create Filter*
- **Select** where you want it to go
- *Create Filter*

To create a rule in Outlook

- **Right click** on a message in your inbox
- Select *Create New Rule*
- **Tap** on presented check boxes, i.e., sender, subject
- **Choose an action** to apply when the conditions are met, i.e., *Move to folder*
- Tap *Create Rule*—select the conditions and actions you want to apply
- Select *Run this rule now* *on messages already in inbox*

> I will create rules or filters for emails I don't need to see but want access to later, automatic notifications, senders I can't unsubscribe from, or messages that don't pertain to me.

Master: Paper Files

You know that guy Justin? Justin Case? He'll monopolize all the real estate in your files and cabinet drawers, scaring you into thinking you have to keep things around. Break up with Justin.

I have very few paper files in my home or office. Between my personal and professional papers, I have one drawer in a file cabinet. That's it. I do have seven years of tax returns and some old journals and sentimental items in my garage, but for the most part, I'm paper-free.

Those insurance documents you have from three years ago? They mean nothing now. Every time your policy renews, throw out the old ones. Bank, credit card, or billing statements? Besides the fact that you can see them online (and more quickly search them that way if you need something) and don't need paper copies delivered anyway (go paperless whenever possible), keeping them is a waste of real estate in your files. Sylvia Inks, Small Business Financial Coach (www.smifinancialcoaching.com), recommends downloading your bank statements to the cloud twice a year, like January 15 and June 15. Some banks only keep digital files for a certain number of months to save room on their servers, so saving your statements to the cloud will give you access to the information if you ever need it. I download mine into **Evernote** as a mindless task twice a year.

If you use paper files, I highly recommend a tickler file system called the SwiftFile, which you can get from the Productive Environment Institute. It's a mobile filing system to remind you of bills due, birthdays, invitations, and appointments as well as to hold your specific paper documents for the exact day you need them. It has 31 different folders for the day of the month and 12 taller folders for the months. After purchase, you can watch tutorials on how to maximize use of the SwiftFile.

Clutter is postponed decisions®. Research shows 80% of what we keep we never use. In the case of paper, that's a conservative estimate! There are only three decisions you can make about any piece of paper: Toss, Act, or File. Always ask, "What is *the worst thing that could happen if I didn't have this piece of paper?" If you can live with your answer, toss, recycle, or shred it! While you may want to keep the papers that still require your action, you can eliminate an enormous amount of paper by converting the documents you want to save for reference into digital form. — **Barbara Hemphill, Founder of Productive Environment Institute**

If you have paper files on your desk, keep the system simple. Add items to an **Action** file if you need to do something with them and a **Reference** file if you'll need them for something coming up soon. Purge on a consistent or routine basis or do what I do and take a photo of it and upload directly into the cloud (again, I use Evernote, but any service will do). With optical character recognition, I can even search for a document I've handwritten and scanned and easily find it in Evernote.

All those cards I get? Unless it is an exceptional card or thank you note, I simply take a photo of it and have a folder in Evernote called *Thank You*. When was the last time you looked at all the cards you saved? I look at my Evernote *Thank You* folder much more frequently than when I kept paper copies.

> *I will purge all outdated or insignificant documents. I will remove duplicate or confusing files and have as few papers as possible. If I use a lot of paper, I will implement a tickler file system. I will kick Justin Case to the curb.*

DECLUTTER: Car

Oof. Raise your hand if this is a problem for you. It's so easy to let our cars become rolling trash bins and receptacles for all kinds of junk we don't really know what to do with. Stop the madness by asking yourself one key question: "Would I be happy to offer my biggest client a ride in my car?" Well, after you work on the next three behavior changes, your answer will likely be yes!

Novice: Trash

Does your car look like a hurricane went through it and left behind debris from two road trips ago? Are you really ever going to pay with that much change in your tray compartment?

Many of us use our cars as a mobile office or unofficial taxi. I decided this year that my car always needed to be client-ready. Would I want a client to get in my car in the state it is in? That's my standard.

The first step is getting rid of that trash that's laying around. A good habit to get into is always to take any trash out as you get out of the car. There is a trash receptacle almost anywhere you park and you probably have one outside your home. Seems simple enough, right? But how many of you have trash on the floor of your car? If you get into a car with trash and drive around with garbage, you are subconsciously telling yourself you are trash. #SorryNotSorry. You're better than that.

> *I will start a habit of always removing any trash from my car every time I get out.*

Pro: *Random Removal*

How many rubber bands, straws, and napkins do you really need? Do you even know what that thing is in your glove compartment (maybe a GPS that suctions to the windshield from back before we all had the Waze app)? Go through your entire car and purge all the excess stuff that has been in there for years and keep one or two of each thing that might come in handy. I used to drive around with about four dollars in change, mostly pennies. I had so many foam earplugs for concerts that I could outfit the entire front row. I had enough napkins to wipe up an oil spill and old insurance and inspection documents from years prior. At least once a quarter, do a purge of anything that has accumulated in your trunk, seatback pockets, and glovebox. Keep a schedule, like the first Sunday of every month or the last day of every quarter, to make sure you don't forget.

> *I will remove all of my excess stuff that I keep just in case (Get out of my car, Justin!) and minimize it to one or two of each. I will do a purge quarterly to stay on top of it.*

Master: *Emergency Kit*

Every car needs a good emergency kit. You can buy these online or make your own. The online kits make it easy because they are typically compact and encased for convenience. The website **www.bugoutbagacademy.com** has a great list of "must haves." I know what you're asking—but I just purged my car of all the extra stuff and now you want me to fill it back up? You don't need five pens, 32 napkins, and whatever that thing was under your seat (some kind of flare gun?) in case of an emergency. A car emergency kit can have all the items stored in an organized bag or tote so you can find what you need when you need it.

Something often forgotten is hangry snacks. Have non-perishable, non-melt, non-freeze hangry snacks for when you have a blood sugar emergency (or you just want to stop and get whatever chemically-concocted gas station delicacy you can find). Foods like raw nuts, dried fruit, and high-quality jerky can be great hangry snacks to keep in your car no matter what your climate. One thing to avoid is plastic bottled water. Cars sitting in the sun can get so hot that the heat can cause the chemicals in plastic bottles to leach into the water. Ew.

> *I will buy or create a car emergency kit.*

HEALTH: Sugar

Okay, now we're getting into the harder stuff. If you've breezed through some of the other behavior changes so far, this one might stop you cold in your tracks. But I know you can do this! Remember, just take one step at a time. Start with the Novice level and work your way up. Go at your own pace.

Novice: One Less Pump

Sugar is everywhere. Besides the obvious places, it's in condiments, yogurt, cereals, granola and energy bars, pasta sauce, salad dressings, flavored creamers, instant oatmeal (instant anything), and frozen entrees. Nutrition labels that have syrup (corn syrup, maple syrup) and words ending in "-ose" (fructose, sucrose, maltose, dextrose) are all different ways of saying "sugar." The more sugar we eat, the more sugar we want. Our taste buds get used to the sweetness of the food and crave more of it.

When we eat sugar, our body responds by releasing insulin from our pancreas to absorb the excess glucose in the blood and stabilize our blood sugar. Your brain secretes dopamine (similar to what happens when you receive notifications on your phone, see Month One) and serotonin, the feel-good hormones. Later, when your blood sugar drops and you get that crash response, it's because the body is releasing stress hormones, which makes us feel worse and crave more sugar.

I was a total sugar addict. Sugar was a food group in my household. We ate giant bowls of ice cream every evening when I was a kid, and at big family functions, we sometimes still have more desserts on the table than entrees and sides. Before I made this change, I had to have a sweet treat every night. If it wasn't chemical-filled, sugar-free, and artificially sweetened, it was sugar-loaded. I knew the most critical behavior change I could make nutritionally was to decrease my sugar intake. I started with one less pump.

I frequently traveled for business and the first stop in any airport was for a peppermint mocha frappe or latte. A grande has six pumps of syrup or the equivalent of ⅓ of a cup (or 68 grams) of sugar. Even the light version is a sugar nightmare at four tablespoons (or 50 grams). Because I was so used to the sweet taste, there was no way I could go to a straight latte or iced coffee, so I asked for one less pump. If the drink had six pumps, I asked for five. Each month I cut back one pump until now I might have a pump on the weekend as a treat, but most of the time, I just have a plain latte or iced coffee with cream or almond milk. And no, the "skinny" version is not the alternative. In fact, it's hard to find out what they put in their sugar-free syrups to make them taste sweet (spoiler alert: it's chemicals). Please, for the love of baby goats, do not eat artificial sweeteners!

Not a coffee drinker? Is sugary yogurt your jam (because that's pretty much what that "fruit" is)? Get a container of plain yogurt and use five ounces of sweetened yogurt and one ounce of the plain version. Gradually decrease the sweetened yogurt until you are eating mostly plain. Love your sweetened instant oatmeal? Mix in plain rolled oats a little at a time until you are ready to move on to steel-cut oats. Find one thing you can combine to have less of the sugar and more of the unadulterated, wholesome stuff.

Visual aides are always helpful too. Put nine teaspoons of sugar in a bowl to see how much is in that can of soda. I am notorious for putting ⅓ of a cup of sugar in one bowl and then pouring it slowly into another during presentations to demonstrate how much sugar I once was consuming daily *just in my latte*. The gasps in the audience are audible every single time. Do this for a few of your favorite foods and that action alone might be enough to make a difference in what you choose. It's also a great exercise to do with kids to show them the difference in sugar content for different foods.

As a membership director at a business club, I get unlimited wine. I don't want to give up wine, but I do want to drink less. I'm going to ask the servers to only give me a little bit each time they come by, rather than filling my glass, so I don't have to say no but will ultimately drink less .— Ashley Melville

I will get less sugar in _____ **by replacing it with or adding** _____.

Pro: Artificial Sweeteners

As I mentioned earlier, if I could advise a person only one thing to do to improve their nutrition, I would ask them to avoid artificial sweeteners like the plague. But I know how tough it can be to eliminate them. I used to be a Diet Mountain Dew and Crystal Light junkie. Entire books and documentaries have been created on how bad artificial sweeteners are for you. In a nutshell, they have multiple negative effects on the body and brain.

- *The Canadian Medical Association Journal* analyzed 37 studies and 400,000 people over ten years. They found that long-term use of artificial sweeteners didn't lead to weight loss, and people who regularly consumed them were actually at *higher risk* for weight gain, obesity, diabetes, and heart disease.[1]

Don't think you're tricking your brain by using artificial sweeteners. You'll still release insulin because your mind thinks your body is eating sugar. Also, since artificial sweeteners are so much sweeter than real sugar, your body gets used to it and will continue to crave sweet things. Once I removed artificial sweeteners, I stopped craving sugar. Imagine! Artificial sweeteners include aspartame (NutraSweet and Equal), sucralose (Splenda), acesulfame potassium, neotame, and saccharin (Sweet'N Low).

But wait, what about stevia? It's natural, right? Stevia can be a better alternative if it's the actual plant, but most stevia on the market is processed and contains added erythritol from corn, dextrose, or other artificial sweeteners (Truvia is an example). If you must use it, try growing it yourself and eating it in plant or leaf form or make tinctures out of it but avoid the white processed and powdered versions.

> *I will eliminate artificial sweeteners from my meal plan. I will do this by replacing _____ with _____.*

If you are an artificial sweetener junkie, try replacing one thing at a time, like sugar-free yogurt for real yogurt. Then change something else, until you have replaced all of your regular foods.

Master: Sugar Boundaries

For me, sugar is a slippery slope. If I eat it too often, I'll crave it. If I make excuses for why I can eat it, I will continue to find more. I like Gretchen Rubin's theory that some people are abstainers and others are moderators. Abstainers need to say no to something (sometimes forever) and have clear rules. Gray areas send them down the slope. Moderators may overeat or obsess over what they can't have until they give in and eat more than they would have to begin with. To have boundaries with sugar (or whatever your vice is—alcohol, trans-fats, fried foods, etc.), I've come up with boundary suggestions for abstainer and moderator personalities.

Abstainers: My own rules are simple. I only eat sweets on the weekends and holidays. These have to be real holidays that I observe, by the way, not Columbus Day or National Mad Hatters Day. Best friend Lisa's birthday? Yes! Cake for a guy I'm friendly with at the office or know through networking whose wife is having a baby? No. If I wouldn't have them over for dinner, their celebrations are definitely not a holiday for me. This relieves the decision-fatigue of thinking about that cookie or piece of cake and whether I'm going to have it. If it's Monday through Thursday or Friday before eleven a.m., then the answer is no. And yes, I even do this on vacation because a week-long vacation can completely derail a habit that works for me and that I like about myself. I still stick to the weekend and holiday rule. And no, I never feel deprived. Based on your life style, come up with your own rules.

Moderators: If you're used to a sweet treat every afternoon or evening, cut back to one or cut the serving in half.

Other boundaries could be:

- Only eat sweets with other people—This is also a great boundary if alcohol is your vice.

- Don't eat gas station candy—If you can buy it in a gas station, it's not good enough for you. Instead only go for tasty, high-quality treats like gourmet dark chocolate from the specialty confection store you only visit a couple times a year or only those that are homemade by your grandma or favorite aunt (not by you). #TrueStory—I had a client who told me she snacked on her son's Tootsie Rolls, SweetTarts, and Halloween candy at night. I looked at the beautiful, high-powered vice president sitting in front of me and said, "You are worth more than gas station candy." Be the VP of your health and treat your sweet tooth with respect.

- Have only one sweet per day or per meal—This could be a boundary at holidays or parties where there are multiple options. If you have four cakes to choose from, decide on the one you really want.

Prepare and plan for holidays and vacations when you might be tempted or might fall off the wagon. If you decide or are afraid you are going to swim in the sugar seas, plan how you will restart or set dates for when you will remove the leftover offending treats.

> *I will decrease my sugar consumption (or vice of choice) by implementing these boundaries* _____.

I recommend one boundary at a time.

Example: If sweets are a strong daily habit for you, start with gas station candy for a month and then change to eating sweets only with other people and then only on the weekends to decrease your sweet consumption.

REFERENCES IN THIS CHAPTER

[1] http://www.cmaj.ca/content/189/28/E929

MONTH THREE

PRODUCTIVITY:
Email Boundaries

You know that email that you get on Friday at 4:55 p.m. requesting you do something before the nine a.m. meeting on Monday—the one that ruins your weekend? You have my permission (not that you need it) to create boundaries for yourself around emails like this. And if you've been known to send emails like this, make today the day you STOP. Seriously.

Novice: Work Offline

Working offline is a productivity hack to prevent you from getting distracted by emails that are continuing to arrive in your inbox when you're processing what's already there. It allows you to catch up, decreases inappropriate responses, and just plain saves time.

Working offline in Outlook means to click the box *Work*

Offline. No new emails will come in and emails you compose will sit in the outbox until you unclick *Work Offline.* If you install **Boomerang for Outlook,** you can pause your email certain times of the day.

In Gmail, you can activate *Work Offline* mode or do what I do and use the extension **Inbox When Ready** or **Inbox Pause.** Both of these allow you to send emails without seeing any new ones come in unless you click the box to show your inbox or you unpause it on a set schedule that you have determined.

> *I'm paused and actually surprised by what a big difference it made—immediately. My brain is less crazy.* — **Sara Shelp, VP of Accounting**

Working offline and not responding to emails immediately changes the conversation. Have you noticed that when you reply (aka react) right away and the recipient realizes you are currently online, a discussion develops back and forth? Email starts to become like an instant messaging program, and you feel rude if you don't reply again right away because they know you are online.

The way I changed my behavior from being always online and checking email all day long was by working offline and only downloading my emails every hour. I would work offline until I had processed what was currently there. The anxiety was pretty intense at first. I felt like I was missing something or I was doing something illegal or sneaky. I gradually decreased my syncing and sending until I was only doing it four times each day when I worked in corporate. For six years as a business owner, I've looked at my inbox twice daily and no one has ever accused me of not responding quickly enough.

Remember, we teach people how reactive we are. I've taught people I don't live in my inbox.

If you are already thinking, "But my company is different, and it's the culture here," know that you can gradually influence that culture. If you are in a position of hierarchy, people will feel compelled to handle their email as you do. It may take retraining and setting new expectations, but individuals, teams, and companies can move from a reactive culture to a responsive culture.

Working offline is my default, but your job may entail something different. You can start by choosing certain times of the day or a specific number of times per day that you go offline.

Example: For the first and last 30 minutes of email processing time every day, I will work offline. After lunch, I work offline for one hour.

> *My inbox was a disaster, and the constant influx of messages was overwhelming. I felt compelled to immediately address every new email, but Marcey taught me how to set boundaries and create specific working hours. She helped me manage my schedule and readjust my contacts' response time expectations. This has reduced my stress level and increased my proficiency ten-fold. — Lisa Wood, Artist and Singer*

I will process email offline _____ times per day or at _____ and _____ times.

Pro: Processing Like a Task

I don't like the term "checking" email because it sounds passive. Processing email is very different from simply checking your inbox. When you process email, you don't open, read, close it, and tell yourself you'll deal with it later. Processing email means to start at the top or in some other systematic way and go through the threads. Processing means to look at it like any other task, and instead of switchtasking back and forth all day, you consciously go into your inbox at set intervals or times to actually deal with what needs your attention.

The average person sends and receives 124 emails a day.[1] Let's figure out how to process email and get you out of your inbox!

Email processing doesn't mean jumping around out of order unless there is a really urgent requirement that needs your attention. Remember, this is your focused email processing time! Schedule it just like anything else. Set the intention *I am going to process email for the next 25 minutes.* Thinking of it as processing emails, rather than responding to or checking emails, helps to change your mindset since every email requires one of five actions: Delete, Delegate, Reply, Archive, or create a Task (DDRAT). The goal here is to OHIO or Only Handle It Once. Notice that in DDRAT there isn't an option for *leave it in my inbox*. If you can tell by the subject line you can't do anything with it right now, don't even bother opening it yet.

- **Delete** – Delete the email when you can tell by the subject line it's not worth opening or delete after reading it because it's not worth saving

- **Delegate** – Forward to an assistant, coworker, spouse, or whoever needs to take ownership of the task

- **Reply** – Do it if it will take you less than two minutes (don't come back to it later)

- **Archive** – Read and file in a folder (if Outlook) or Archive in Gmail (which will send it to All Mail)

- **Task** – Move it out of your inbox into a task list

> *I treat email like a task to be handled, instead of a means of procrastination. I know when I go into my email, I'm going to use the OHIO (Only Handle It Once) method to respond to what I can and leave the rest until I accomplish my most important priorities for the day. This has really boosted my productivity.* — **Emily Crookston, *The Pocket PhD***

> *The concept of OHIO has changed the way I organize my day and allowed me to re-allocate my time to be more productive. I went from spending at least two to three hours daily managing an ongoing email box of 75 to 100 emails to 30 minutes to one hour per day cleaning up my inbox to under ten emails. Deciding up front and immediately as to what should be deleted, delegated, or tasked has allotted time for me to focus on the actual tasks themselves. I also spend my newly free time focusing on ways to continuously improve my team's culture and performance.* — **Terri Cutshall, *Associate Director***

The order of email processing can change. I would suggest if you are coming back from a vacation or more than a couple of days away, start with the newest first. Why? Because the older ones may already have worked themselves out and you don't want to waste any time working on something complete. If you reply to an older email first, you may find new information in a more recent email that would have changed your reply. Make sure you have your settings on *Conversation View* to ensure you aren't reading outdated emails.

If this is your first time processing email or if you fell off the wagon and need to get back on, set a timer for 25 minutes. Go offline and do something with every single email. Don't waste decisions by continuing to go back to them. Email is another person's agenda or task list. Work offline as much as you can. Staying online and having more emails come in while you are processing the current ones is distracting.

What if your inbox currently has 6,000 read and 800 unread emails? My recommendation is to declare bankruptcy. Archive all of them, except for what has come in the last week or previous day. If you're brave and feeling frisky, just drag in everything except the current day's emails. Don't panic. They're still there and searchable. If they were essential, you would have responded or done something with them, right? You can name this folder whatever you want—it doesn't matter. Most of the emails are probably outdated and you don't need to do anything with them anyway. And if something is really old and you may have dropped the ball—call the sender or get off your butt and go talk to them (if you're in the same office) and find out if the matter is still relevant. Start clean and work your way up from a week ago or even one day ago. Anything older is archived. Give yourself a fresh start. If you start with the old messages, then the ones from today are already old by tomorrow. As Barbara Hemphill of the Productive Environment Institute says, "Clutter is Postponed Decisions®" and that includes email clutter.

When considering your processing, think about your schedule. Is it realistic to schedule email work at specific time intervals such as ten a.m., two p.m., and four p.m.? Or do you need triggers like after your first meeting, after lunch, or two hours before you go home? Whatever time you choose, avoid the first and last thirty minutes of your day. Often people do the opposite and check first and last thing, yet the priority order is all wrong—unless the most important part of your job and your highest value at your company is to be in your inbox. The absolute worst thing you can do is open your email as your first task. One little email can derail your whole routine and plan for your day.

I agree with almost everything in the *Four-Hour Work Week* by Tim Ferriss. One thing I disagree with, however, is using an out-of-office responder saying when you process emails. I don't care when you process, and now I have to delete your out-of-office message every time. If you give specific times, people will expect you to respond at those times. My process for the last six years has been to process twice a day and for less than an hour. That's it. If I need to send emails out throughout the day, I do. If I need to see if someone has replied, I use the search and type in their name; otherwise, I'm offline and doing important things for my business outside of my inbox.

> *I will process email as a task* _____
> *times per day or at approximately these times*
> _____.

Master: Delay Send

I am obsessed with delaying my emails. With *Delay Send*, I can write the email as I'm thinking about it but postpone the send until a later time. When and why would I want to do this?

- *For emails that require a decision like signing a contract or reviewing a proposal* – I want the recipient to get that email at a strategic time. For instance, I don't send these early in the morning when they feel they have a load of stuff on their plates and my email may get pushed back. I don't send at the end of the day when they are tired and may resort to a status-quo or fear-based decision (answering no). I also don't send important emails on Friday afternoons and usually not on Mondays.

- *For emails in the evenings or on the weekends when I might be working but I don't want to steal someone else's evening* – Realize that if you are in a hierarchical position, your staff will feel compelled to respond to you if you email them at 9:22 p.m. or on a Sunday. It doesn't matter how many times you tell them you don't expect them to. Ideally, they wouldn't be looking at email then anyway, but they might not have this book to know it's not productive.

  Note: I understand some people enjoy or must work at night and weekends. You can consider whatever their "off-hours" might be instead.

- *For people who are on vacation or traveling when it might get lost* – These emails I send the day after they return.

- *For follow-up emails I don't want to forget to send* – I can schedule these emails out days, weeks, or even months.

- *To stop an email thread from going back and forth like a conversation* – I will even delay sending my response for ten minutes because I'm more than likely going to have moved on from email by then and can wait until my next processing time to take care of any response.

Here are some other apps and services that I recommend to my clients:

Besides Delay Send, Gmail has the **Boomerang** service, which can boomerang emails back to you at a specified time, delay a response, and remind you to follow up. **RightInbox** is free software that allows you to *send now*, *send later*, or *remind me*. I use **Streak CRM** for all of these things. It is my Client Relationship Management system of choice.

In Outlook, you have to click *Delay Send* and then schedule a specific time. It isn't nearly as fast, but it's doable. You might want to work offline instead and then just sync and send during work hours. If your company allows it, install **Boomerang for Microsoft Outlook** to make it simple.

Vynamic is a forward-thinking company that has posted email guidelines on their website. Employees are encouraged not to send emails in the evenings, on weekends, or on Vynamic-observed holidays. People can work whenever they want, but they can't send emails during off-hours. My business and the businesses of my entrepreneurial clients aren't the typical nine-to-five set-up. Sometimes I work on Saturdays to spread out my work during the week or because I want to run errands or do "Saturday Stuff" on a weekday. I also like the quiet of working a little on Saturday. When I remember (because sometimes they sneak past me, and I don't realize until it's too late), I pause my outgoing emails to be sent on Monday or Tuesday. The fewer emails people have to read on the weekend, the better.

"No Friday or evening emails makes no sense.
My company is global!"

I received this feedback from a workshop attendee at a large international corporation. If you are dealing with people overseas and their ten a.m. is your eight p.m., you're right, it may not matter. The point is to consider who is receiving the email and their own time zone. People will always use the excuse, "If I'm not working at night with everyone else, I can't keep up," without realizing that they are actually a part of the problem. If you operate a nine-to-five job, then your evening or early morning should be your time. I work in the evenings sometimes, but I may also take a break in the afternoon. My schedule isn't a typical corporate schedule. Feel free to use these tips to set the boundaries that work best for you and your situation.

Some companies have "No Email Fridays." It's a movement where no email can be sent internally on Friday or, at a minimum, after noon on Friday. This may be challenging for many companies, but I'm sure people could get used to calling more and emailing less on Fridays. This is a movement—people don't want the Friday Dump. Receiving an email late in the day on Friday with a deliverable for Monday or anything that will make you shut down your computer and stress about it over the weekend is considered a "dump." Maybe it isn't realistic, but one thing to consider is whether you would call a person and ask them to do something at the same time you are sending an email asking for it. For example, would you call someone on Friday at six p.m. or Saturday at ten a.m. and request they create a new presentation for you? Probably not, but somehow emailing the request seems culturally acceptable. I think saving that email until the new workweek is more appropriate, and it lets people enjoy their weekends. If you want to work, that's fine, but you shouldn't expect others to work unless their job is to work on weekends. Schedule it to send on Monday.

Another reason companies have instituted a ban on Friday emails is that they want people to communicate with each other—by voice (what a concept)! At U.S. Cellular, "No Email Fridays" were initially met with resistance but soon became not only acceptable but appreciated. Employees got to know each other better and in one instance, two people who thought they were communicating across the country were on the same floor in the same building! Other companies banning Friday emails include PBD Worldwide Fulfillment, which dropped their email volume *75 percent* and E-Verifile that only allows email on external communications on Fridays. They believe this policy results in a happier workforce and better communication.

If you think that a phone call takes more time than an email, consider how long some threads are that could have been completed in one minute or less over the phone. Make a rule for yourself and start with your team. Try calling or physically speaking to a team member on Fridays. Then stretch this out to your department and later to the rest of your company. Who knows, you may even get your weekend back too!

> *I will delay sending emails at _____.*

Example: I will delay sending work-related emails at night or on weekends.

DECLUTTER:
Newsletters and Promotions

We all have extra papers and digital junk mail just laying around collecting real or virtual dust. In this section, you'll learn some clever ways to clear out the junk and avoid bringing it into your world at all. Good-bye valueless newsletters and promotions!

Novice: Paper Junk Mail

I can't stand junk mail, and I think it should be illegal for credit card companies to send out applications. If you want a credit card, you can go online to get one. Sending unsolicited offers to my door only makes me a target for people to steal my identity. The less paper mail you receive, the less you will have to contend with, and the less waste will end up in your recycle bin. A few simple online forms can help you get control of your paper.

Nancy Haworth of **On Task Organizing** states that the most common thing she sees people keep in a kitchen that they don't need or use is paper. Often paper and mail will fill up space on the kitchen counters and inside kitchen drawers.

When decluttering a kitchen, try to designate one place for these documents, preferably in an area far from where cooking takes place (hello, fire hazard!) or in another area of the home such as an entryway or home office.

DMAChoice.org (Direct Marketing Association) is a free mail preference service where you can opt out of junk mail via email. If you don't want any catalogs, magazines, or other mail offers, you can opt out of that category entirely. It also allows you to register someone who is deceased or register as a caretaker. Unfortunately, there is no opt-out for political ads.

CatalogChoice.org is complementary to DMAChoice if you only want to opt out of specific magazines and catalogs. A great feature is the ability to opt-down instead of opt-out. You might want the Victoria's Secret catalogue quarterly instead of weekly for example. The site can do that for companies that will allow it.

OptOutPreScreen.com allows you to electronically opt out of receiving credit card mail for five years or opt-out permanently by writing a letter. I only have one credit card that I use for personal purchases and two for my business. I've frozen all three of the accounts to protect myself from identity theft. Freezing means a credit card can't be opened in my name without me unfreezing or thawing the account. It only takes a few minutes to thaw if I need a new credit card. If you're someone who opens up new cards all the time to save ten percent or you have an issue with your credit, it may be worthwhile to perform this step to set yourself up for success and make it difficult for you to continue this habit.

Paper Karma is an app for your phone. Just snap a photo of the envelope with the *Sender* and *Recipient* in focus, and they will contact the mailer to have you removed from the distribution list.

> *What works well for our family is dealing with mail as soon as it enters the house. I immediately recycle the junk mail without even opening it. We have a decorative hanging wall file in our foyer – one slot for mail that we need to deal with and the other for receipts. It's been a lifesaver for getting rid of piles of mail in the kitchen. — Mary-Lynn Fulton*

I will complete opt-outs for my junk mail, magazines, and other offers I don't want and freeze or opt-out of the credit card offers.

Pro: Digital Junk Mail

Junk email can be a distraction and a way to procrastinate. I hardly have any junk coming into my inbox because I stay on top of it by not subscribing unnecessarily, opting out of communications any time I am new to a website, unsubscribing right away, and using a filtering service. As I discussed before, a filter service keeps emails from hitting your inbox by allowing you to easily unsubscribe or roll them up into a once-daily digest. Unsubscribing using this method sends those emails to a "black hole," which means you aren't really unsubscribing. Instead, you just aren't seeing them. This is great if you know someone with a newsletter you don't want to receive and you are afraid it will offend them if you were to unsubscribe. I mentioned **Unroll.Me** and **Sanebox** as two filtering options in Month Two. They also apply well here.

Some people create a rule or filter (for help with this, see Month Two) so that any email that has the word *unsubscribe* in it bypasses their inbox and goes straight to Trash or another folder that they choose to check on their own time. Be careful with this one though because you may miss some crucial communications. Do a quick scan weekly to see if there is something you need to address.

> *I will sign up for a filtering service or create a rule or filter that any email with the word unsubscribe will bypass my inbox or go into a folder if I want to scan it after I've processed all my important email.*

Master: Save Yourself from Your Whims

Another benefit of cutting down on unnecessary marketing communications is that it can also save you money. If you have an issue with buying more than you need to online, don't register for an account when buying something. I got this idea from Gretchen Rubin's book *Outer Order, Inner Calm.* Choose the guest option instead so that you don't get added to a list for promotions. When I started doing this, I noticed I bought way less. One of my weaknesses is Amazon, and it is a total time suck for me. Opting out of all of their communications really helped me curb spending on a whim after clicking on one of their ads.

> *I will register as a guest or will opt-out of email communications immediately when purchasing something so that I don't get sucked into buying things I don't need.*

HEALTH: Movement Opportunities

This is one of my favorite sections. I love to exercise, but I know it's not everyone's favorite thing and for some, it's really hard to find the time to work out for an hour during a typical work day. That's exactly why I developed what I like to call "Movement Opportunities." These are quick and easy ways to make time to move your body for short bursts throughout your day. And bonus, you don't even have to change your clothes to see a benefit!

Novice: Movement Opportunities at Home

For me a day without exercise is like a day without brushing my teeth or washing my face. It just doesn't feel right. However, not everyone likes to exercise. Even if you happen to like exercising, the 45 minutes you run in the morning or the hour you walk or go to the gym at night might not be enough to counteract sitting all day. **NEAT — Non-Exercise Activity Thermogenesis** is the calorie burn we get from doing everyday activities that we often don't consider exercise. I like to think of these as Movement Opportunities or bursts of movement throughout the day that can last anywhere from a few seconds to a few minutes. Besides being a mega stress reliever, Movement Opportunities can give you energy.

Regular and non-regular exercisers can look for Movement Opportunities to increase their energy, strength, improve their sleep, and decrease their stress, all without taking up too much time or breaking a sweat. They can be 30 seconds, two minutes, or ten minutes. Never underestimate what a quick two to three-minute routine can do for your stress levels and energy. Will it get you a six-pack? No. But it will improve your mood and your health.

I like to find a trigger, something I do consistently every day, and create a Movement Opportunity before, during, or after that trigger. To see how I used a litterbox as a trigger, visit **https://youtu.be/HpREmWVhA9k.** Natural triggers are brushing your teeth, taking medication, brewing coffee, showering, letting the dog out, or feeding a pet. These are all things you would do every day and are consistent triggers.

My client Nikki, a frequent business traveler, has a mantra, "Open the door and hit the floor." As soon as she gets to a hotel, before touching her phone, her laptop, or eating the dinner she brought with her to the room, she puts a towel down on the floor to do ten minutes of Pilates or yoga.

My client Michelle didn't like exercise and swore she didn't have time for it. We needed to reframe her mindset. Instead of thinking of exercise in terms of putting on different clothes, getting sweaty, and having to redo her hair and makeup, we framed it as Movement Opportunities. I gave her five 5-minute workouts she could do between client appointments, using what she already had in her workspace, without getting sweaty, and even while wearing a skirt. Every day she would have between one and five opportunities for this kind of mini-workout. That was five to 25 minutes of exercise (sneaky!) every day that she wouldn't have achieved without this new regime. And she no longer thought of exercise as a changing clothes event. After a few months, she sent a text saying, "I think my butt's getting higher just from opportunities!" It's one of my favorite texts. Now she loves actual workouts and has an entirely different outlook on exercise.

> *Working with Marcey made me change the way I feel about exercise and making it part of my life. I went from rolling out of bed with just enough time to eat and shower and get to work to taking time in the morning to move before anything else. It has changed the course of my day!* — ***Michelle Scaraglino, Stylist***

An audience member at one of my keynotes relayed a Movement Opportunity I recommend for when you are sitting at stop lights to her grandpa. Many of us are getting "tech neck" or a forward-head leaning posture from looking down at small devices. This contributes to headaches as well as neck and shoulder pain. To strengthen these weak neck muscles, I do this simple exercise while waiting at a stop light: with my chin level, I push my head into the seat headrest and hold. My audience member's grandpa started doing this in the car and at home. About a year later, he was in a car accident that resulted in his car being totaled and his airbag deploying. He had no neck injury and attributed this to the neck-strengthening exercises he had been doing.

> *I will use _____ as my trigger and perform _____ . This will be my new Movement Opportunity at home.*

Pro: Movement Opportunities at Work

You've probably heard the phrase "sitting is the new smoking." The adverse health effects of sitting are extraordinary and shouldn't be taken lightly. If you are a professional sitter, you risk a decrease in health, quality of life, and productivity—not to mention that you may end up with a case of butt amnesia. Butt or gluteal amnesia is common among people who sit all day. The gluteal muscles forget how to fire from lack of use. This leads to lower back, hip, knee, and ankle pain. Prolonged sitting has been linked to:

- High blood pressure and cholesterol
- Increased insulin production after just one day of sitting, which could lead to diabetes
- Higher risk for colon, breast, and endometrial cancers
- Weak abdominals, tight hip flexors, and weak glutes
- Poor leg circulation, varicose veins, and deep vein thrombosis
- Weak bones
- Slower brain function
- Neck Strain
- Sore shoulders and back

Standing and sit-stand desks should be an option for everyone. It pains me when my clients have to submit a medical request to get a standing desk, especially when a Varidesk costs as little as $275. It's much more acceptable now, but companies that want you to wait until you have health issues to spring for a sit-stand desk have it so bass-ackward I don't even know how to process that policy. One of my clients was pregnant, had back issues, and even after a medical note from her doctor, still didn't get approval for an appropriate desk! At the new headquarters of the *News & Observer* in Raleigh, North Carolina, everyone has a sit-stand desk, and it's normal to see people adjusting throughout the day. When they moved locations, leaders at the news publication made sure it was non-negotiable that everyone have this option.

When the News & Observer was working on the design of our new workspace, a key consideration was designing for many needs. Our staff spans generations and our work requires very different activities for each staff member throughout the day. A reporter might need to collaborate with colleagues, then have quiet head-down writing, then have social media time. Our administrative and advertising teams can spend hours on video calls with remote-location colleagues and clients. We needed flexibility for all of this. Part of that strategy was to provide sit-to-stand desks for every member of our staff. It allows our team members to break up long periods of heads-down or video conference work where you can't leave your desk with standing breaks. It gives our team members control over their work environment. We also provide many huddle spaces, sofas, high tops, and small one-person phone rooms so each staff member can find the area they need for the work they are doing at that moment. A healthy workspace requires that we consider how our staff works throughout the day, who they interact with and what technology they use. We've created an environment that provides maximum flexibility. — Sara Glines Kilpatrick, President & Publisher, News & Observer

I also have clients embarrassed to stand because no one else in their office does it. I'm guessing in about five years the professional sitters will be the ones being stared at. Back when I bought my desk about ten years ago, the options were minimal. I had to go for a medical cart on wheels that works perfectly and has five shelves for me to house my computer, lamp, printer, and peripherals. I'm so used to standing that I look for opportunities everywhere. When I'm at a coffee shop or the airport, I look for a high-top table where I can stand. The airports that have actual standing areas or even treadmill desks (Go Minneapolis Airport!) are putting the health and productivity of their passengers first.

There is a plethora of options today, ranging from do-it-yourself (DIY) solutions like stacking your computer on books or bringing in a piece of wood with legs to place on top of your regular desk to higher-end solutions like $3,000 desks on hydraulics. The Varidesk is nice because you can use it for sitting and standing. The versatility enables you to choose based on how you feel, and the price range of $275–$650 is reasonable.

My portable traveling desk of choice is the StandStand. The StandStand, $69–$99, comes in Baltic Birch or Bamboo in three different sizes depending on the user's height. It weighs less than two pounds and entirely collapses to the size of a laptop. I can fit my StandStand, laptop, peripherals, and everything else I need in my backpack.

If you purchase a standing desk, start using it in short intervals, 15 to 25 minutes at a time. If you wear high-heels, take them off. One of my clients had back pain after she went all out and stood most of the day as soon as she got her desk.

Your body needs to get used to standing and maintaining good posture. Standing desks aren't a cure-all. Just like you can be a potato chip vegan or a bologna-eating paleo, you can also be a slumped over, hip-cocked stander.

A treadmill or bike desk or an under-the-desk elliptical would be a little more advanced than a standing desk. If you go for one of these, commit to doing specific tasks using the machine, since sometimes the movement can be distracting. The idea is not to break a sweat but still get a good workout in. Slowly walk or lightly pedal so it isn't distracting. I have my **Fit Bike** on my screened in porch and use it to watch webinars or read. I rarely break a sweat, but it is definitely a movement I wouldn't be getting standing at my desk or sitting in a chair.

Other ideas for Movement Opportunities at work:

- Do 15 counter push-ups in the bathroom before you wash your hands

- Do five chair squats before you process email

- Squeeze your pelvic floor with kegels during the elevator ride (if you have to take the elevator) – Yes, ladies, this is a vital Movement Opportunity too!

- Take the stairs – This seems like a no-brainer, but how many of you actually do it? If you have so many floors it would cause you to get sweaty, just do a few flights and finish the rest on the elevator.

  I look for Movement Opportunities everywhere, even if I'm just standing at my desk! If someone walks by my office and sees me marching in place, I tell them, "I promised Marcey I'd keep this up!" When I travel for business, I make sure to organize the 6:00 a.m. walking club, so we get in our steps before the conference starts. I incorporated a no excuses policy for myself. I don't have to commit to huge amounts of exercise, but I have to do something. Even if I don't feel well, I can do something and usually end up doing more than I think I will. — **Deb McMurray, Contract Operations**

> **I will use** _____ **as my trigger to perform** _____. **This will be my Movement Opportunity at work.**

Master: Walking Meetings

If you want to be one of the cool kids, perform walking meetings. Walking meetings work best with two or three people and have been shown to increase creativity, collaboration, and encourage openness in conversation. Getting away from your office space and out into nature can also boost creativity and productivity. Walking side-by-side may decrease intimidation too and the real or perceived hierarchy that comes with sitting across from someone at a desk.

Guidelines for walking meetings:

- Make sure it's an area you know – This is not the time for exploring or getting lost.

- Consider the time of day and weather – July at one p.m. in North Carolina or any time of day in February in Minnesota may not be ideal walking times.

- Ask the person ahead of time if they are okay with a moving meeting – Don't surprise them when they are wearing a three-piece suit or three-inch heels.

- Keep it short and slow – This is not the time to show your physical prowess or prove how fast you can walk a mile. Check in about the pace and be mindful of their breathing to ensure they aren't dying inside while you are skipping along.

- Some of my clients with direct reports do "walkie talkies" – No, not using actual walkie-talkies, just by phone when they live in different cities. I seldom talk to my family members without walking around my neighborhood. Sitting to talk on the phone actually feels weird to me.

Ideal walking meetings are with friends, one-on-ones with your manager, meetings with referral partners, or sales calls, especially if you know the person is interested in their health. **One owner of a credit card processing company who had attended one of my workshops, closed a $1 million+ deal during one walking meeting.** If you want to be memorable, you'll do something besides coffee, lunch, or drinks.

> *I've always loved brainstorming with others to solve challenges and come up with new business ideas. Marcey's plan to have a walking meeting—instead of my traditional sit-around-a-table session—was a refreshing and energizing change of pace. I was able to work through a challenge that had been plaguing me for two years, and I am now implementing a solution to serve a new market.* **— Nika Stewart, CEO, Streambank Media**

I will commit to doing _____ walking meetings per week or I will commit to doing _____ as walking meetings.

REFERENCES IN THIS CHAPTER

[1] https://frontapp.com/blog/2018/07/20/
     how-much-time-are-you-spending-on-email/

MONTH FOUR

PRODUCTIVITY: Email Writing

How many of the emails you write are actually unnecessary? We could all cut down on the number of emails we send and receive if we put a stop to unnecessary email messages, created better subject lines, and took some time out to write canned emails for scenarios that come up over and over. In this section, we focus on streamlining our email writing.

Novice: Thanks! Okay! Got it!

One of my pet peeves is receiving a timewaster email of *Thanks!* as an acknowledgment when I don't need it. It's just an email I have to delete. If someone goes above and beyond, for example, stays late at work to get a required signature, I will email back and thank them (with a message that is more heartfelt than "Thanks!"). However, if someone is just doing their regular job, I don't respond back. When I used to be a manager, I asked my staff not to reply with *thanks* emails unless I did something above and beyond what I should be doing. If

I didn't go out of my way to do whatever they were thanking me for, I wouldn't have even noticed if they didn't thank me!

How many people would actually notice if someone didn't write back a *thanks* email for routine things? Who has gone to bed at night thinking, "I sent that presentation to my manager to review and she didn't reply back to say thanks. I wonder if she got it?" Most of the time, we don't even mean *thank you*. It's just a confirmation or acknowledgment that we received whatever they sent. Some clients may need a *thank you*, but your spouse, sister, or colleague probably doesn't.

It's essential to remember, if it is just an *acknowledgment*, don't do it. I would say the same about throw-away responses like *OK* or *Got it* too. At least since the mid-1990's, email has been reliable enough that we don't need to confirm receipt. The majority of the time, there is no need to acknowledge with a timewaster email.

I never have people asking me if I received their emails because I haven't trained them with email acknowledgments. I also don't do the uber-annoying habit of sending an email and then calling or texting the person to let them know I sent it. That's even worse. We train people how we work and how we respond. Reply in a timely manner, only if a response is required.

When I present a session on email management, without fail, I get a message later that day like this—"I know we aren't supposed to thank you, but that workshop was amazing! I learned how to process my email and prioritize my time so much better than before. I can already see the difference it will make." This *is* the kind of thank you email to send! They are expressing how they feel and being genuine about how I helped them. They aren't just responding to a follow-up from me with an attachment or link I promised and acknowledging they received it.

If you send an email and you don't want a reply, one easy thing you can do is type NRN at the end for "No Reply Necessary." This helps someone know that you don't expect a response, thereby avoiding the *thanks* or *OK* reply. If you email several people but don't want to open up a group discussion, you can state "respond only to sender" at the end, so they know they don't need to *reply all*, another often abused form of email laziness.

> *I will not send timewaster emails as acknowledgments. If I must retrain people on my team, I will let them know that we can curb this habit and trust that the person has received the email.*

Pro: *Subject Lines*

Good subject lines are critical because they help to filter what is important and allow you to search and retrieve emails later and provide a timely response. With a good subject line, you can tell the possible actions needed before opening it.

Writing "Action Requested" or AR and the due date or deadline in the subject line lets a person know that they need to respond or do something by a specific time. When I put this in an email, it tells the person that if they have more urgent needs, they can get to my email later, or it signals that mine is timely and needs to be prioritized.

Example: Action Requested by September 2: Program Questionnaire and Flyer

Writing "NOT URGENT" in the subject line tells the recipient that they can skip opening the email until they have more time. I like to use this when I know someone has been on vacation or is overwhelmed with their workload.

Example: NOT URGENT: Additional photos for content repository

Another one of my pet peeves is the subject line "*Quick Question.*" If it's quick, put the entire question in the subject line. If you can't put it in the subject line, then it is not a quick question. If it's just a one-liner, type it in the subject line followed by EOM or "End of Message." Then they don't have to open up the email. One of my clients did a search for "Quick Question" and 47 (!) emails came up. Not helpful for trying to find an archived email.

Example: Please send Simpson report by Friday 5:00pm. EOM

> *I will be intentional with subject lines and write them in a searchable way.*

Master: *Canned Responses*

If you write the same or a similar email more than five times, stop rewriting and start using an email template, otherwise known as a canned response or snippet depending on the program you are using. Not only will this save you time, it ensures that your answers are consistent. If you have staff managing responses, this method maintains consistency across your department. You can always personalize, but keep in mind, the less you have to write each time, the better.

Items that can be templated include:

- Instructions to begin a project
- Responses to negative feedback or unhappy customers so you aren't emotionally charged when writing back
- Appointment scheduling information
- Instructions for the completion of a task
- Office hours, directions, and logistics
- Frequently asked questions

A few items I have snippets for include:

- Press kit link
- Instructions for Zoom video conferencing
- Instructions for invoicing and scheduling
- Affiliate links
- Testimonial requests
- Directions to my business club
- Instructions for guest posts

In Outlook, the templates capability is a little wonky but worth it for frequently sent emails.

- Start a **New Email**
- In the message window, tap the **File** tab
- Tap **Save As**
- In the **Save As** dialog box, go to the **Save As type** list, tap **Outlook Template**
- In the **File name** box, type the name of your template
- Tap **Save**

In Gmail, you can use canned responses.

- In the compose screen, click the three dots next to the trash can on the far right corner of your screen
- Click **Canned Responses**
- Select your response to insert into your email

I also use **Streak**, which allows me to save templates as **Snippets**.

> *I will set up templates or canned responses for emails that I send frequently.*

DECLUTTER: Bathroom

The bathroom is one of the rooms in your home that you might not think to declutter. Yeah, you think about cleaning out the garage or the shed or the attic or the hall closet. But the bathroom? Well, if you travel, you probably have hotel toiletries you don't need. And if you have regular-size products that you don't use and haven't yet thrown out, what are you waiting for? What about that linen closet?

Novice: Travel-Size Toiletries

A few years ago, I was helping my mom declutter her bathroom and found eight travel-size tubes of toothpaste. She had just bought one for an upcoming trip, not realizing how many she already had. This is a common problem, especially for business travelers or people who vacation frequently. I used to have a bag full of shampoos, conditioners, and body wash that I only used once. It felt wasteful to throw them away at the hotel since they can't reuse them. But if they're just sitting on my shelf at home, they aren't being used either! I like that some hotels are going the more environmentally friendly route of having larger bottles of products for use in the room.

Yes, it can be wasteful, but how old are those travel-size shampoos in your cabinet? If you aren't using them at home and you aren't taking them with you when you travel because you're using the hotel's shampoo, then these products will just keep piling up.

You have three options: (a) take your own toiletries and don't even touch the ones at the hotel or (b) use them at the hotel and then use them at home (gasp!) or 3) give them to a local shelter. This can be a good way to try "samples" of new products, and if it's a product you would never buy, then there's really no reason to keep it around.

Not an option—letting them take up prime real estate in your closet. These products do have a shelf-life and once they are opened, they can start to breed bacteria. Use them up within six months or throw them away.

> *I will stop hoarding travel toiletries and instead will* _____.

Pro: Regular-Size Toiletries

Now that you've purged your travel toiletries, it's time to move on to the big stuff. This might be harder because you paid for these yourself and some may have been expensive (anything you bought at the salon). Take everything out of your cabinet—KonMari style—and count just how many shampoos, lotions, potions, and creams you have. If you are someone who buys whatever product a celebrity is promoting on an infomercial or have a product-addiction, add up how much money you have sitting in front of you and consider the consequences. You've probably bought so much that some of it is outdated, old, unusable, and not worth the money you spent (apparently, since you haven't used it).

As soon as a cream or lotion is opened, it starts to break down, some faster than others. As painful as it might be, toss all the old, expired stuff and use what you have and like. I'm a closer (and not just when it comes to sales!), which means I like to have only one or two things going at a time, and I will finish a product before I open a new one.

Shelf lives:
- Cream makeup, lipstick, and glosses – 12 to 18 months
- Mascara – 3 to 6 months
- Eye and lip pencils – up to 5 years
- Eyeshadow and powders – up to 2 years
- Nail polish and other nail care products – about 2 years before it thickens, separates, and evaporates

- Perfumes and colognes – 3 to 5 years
- Lotions, moisturizers, and other skin care products – 2 to 3 years
- Dental care products – 12 to 18 months
- Hairstyling products – about 18 months

If you have ten lipsticks, it can add to the decision-fatigue in the morning when you are getting ready. Narrow it down to 3 or 4 and make life simpler.

When decluttering a bathroom, some items to quickly declutter are things that have expired. Not only do medications expire, but sunscreen has an expiration date. Although most cosmetics don't have an expiration date, makeup is prone to bacterial contamination, discoloration, and drying out. Some items, such as mascara, should be used within 3 to 6 months. Other cosmetics, such as lipstick, should be used within 2 years. If you have owned any makeup product for more than 2 years, it's time to discard it. — **Nancy Haworth, On Task Organizing**

> **I will throw away all products that are expired or that I can't use within six months.**

Master: *Linens*

I don't know if guests think our house is freezing or if blankets are just an easy gift to give, but at one point we had eight blankets for the two of us. Keeping these around took up prime real estate in our closet and kept someone who really needs them from being warm. We donated four and can use the extras for guests when they visit.

Several years ago I minimized our bedsheets to three sets—one that is currently on our bed, one that is being laundered, and one for guests. That's all we need. At one point, we only had two sets because I just planned to wash and put the sheets back on the same day.

How many sets of sheets and towels can you possibly use? We once had ten bath towels, but since it's just Kevin and me and we usually use a towel twice, we would not go through ten towels before we do laundry each week. I opened up the linen closet real estate for other things.

Do you have an excess of towels, blankets, or linens that could be donated to a shelter for someone who really needs them? Animal shelters also appreciate the items you are storing in your closet.

> *I will consider how many blankets, sheets, and towels I really need and donate the excess or throw away any that are worn or have holes.*

HEALTH: Veggies

If you're not a huge fan of veggies, this section is for you! I didn't think I loved vegetables until I realized I just hadn't been preparing them in ways that would bring out their deliciousness. Once I learned a few of these tricks and tips, I became a veggie-eating master. I know you can do it too. Once you make these behaviors changes, you will be surprised you ever believed you could get along without eating vegetables.

Novice: Hide a Veggie

Earlier in the book, I declared that my family did not eat vegetables growing up. I'm not the only one with this background. The small number of vegetables I did try was in the school cafeteria, and they were never tasty, being either canned or overcooked or (most of the time) both. I can't even count the number of times I've heard people say how much they love (roasted) Brussel sprouts but hated Brussel sprouts growing up because they were either boiled or thawed from frozen. Access helps. Twenty or thirty years ago in the Midwest access was a challenge. Now, living in North Carolina, I can get almost any vegetable year-round due to our climate. Quality food + proper preparation = a whole new world. I'm also lucky to have access to a Community Supported Agriculture Program, **Papa Spuds,** that delivers fresh, local fruits and vegetables to my door every week.

If you have children, please introduce them to plants as a privilege, not as a punishment. Don't just pour green beans from a can and warm them up. Don't cut a tomato in half, plop it on their plate, and make them eat it before they can leave the table (my introduction to tomatoes from my dad and then I didn't eat them for 30 years).

Food researchers at Ohio State University and Cornell University found that children are five times more likely to eat a salad if they have grown some of the vegetables themselves. Get them involved in choosing healthy foods and have them help pick out the plant they want to try for the week.[1]

It's also helpful to take kids to farms, orchards, or farmers markets so they can see where vegetables are grown and who grows them.

Now that I know how to cook them properly, I freakin' love vegetables. As in if you gave me a choice between grilled or roasted peppers and ice cream, I'd get a second helping of grilled peppers. I order Brussel sprouts so often at my business club, the waitstaff knows before I tell them and sometimes have already put in the order. Take a class or watch a YouTube video, but please learn how to properly prepare your veggies. It really can make all the difference!

If you are already a veggie lover, you might skip to the Pro recommendation or even skip this whole month's health habit because you may not need it. But if you're struggling to help those around you become veggie lovers too, read on for some excellent tips that could help them out.

This section is really for the people who are struggling to eat any veggies at all. So, if you are adopting this first monthly habit and know it will be a challenge, it's okay to eat only the vegetables you know, like, and trust at this point. What doesn't count? Potatoes and corn. These are basically starches, and you should think of them as a substitute for bread or pasta. I do count sweet potatoes in moderation, however, because you get a higher nutritional bang for your buck with them.

When I first adopted this "hide a veggie" habit, I wasn't even getting one serving per day. Seriously. I was a carbatarian or a vegetarian who didn't eat vegetables. So I started out with one serving per day and even that was a challenge at first. (How was I even functioning?) After two weeks, I bumped it up to two servings per day for three weeks, then three servings a day for a month. When I got up to four servings a day, which was my goal at the time, I had to stretch that habit out for two months. It was tough because I still wasn't a good cook. One of the things I had to do at the time was "hide a veggie" in something that made it easy to incorporate. To be clear, it's not that you don't know you're eating veggies (after all you're probably preparing the food for yourself). It's that you don't taste them or at least you can live with the difference in taste.

Here are ways to "hide a veggie," which I still do today but not because I need to hide them anymore:

- Frozen spinach or riced cauliflower in my smoothies – Seriously, riced cauliflower is excellent in a smoothie. It adds fiber and is tasteless.

- Riced anything in everything! – Now that riced broccoli, cauliflower, sweet potato, and blends are easily purchased in your freezer section, these are fantastic additions to soups and stews. I even added some to potato soup for my family and no one noticed.

- Riced veggies in eggs

- Riced veggies in chicken or tuna salad

- Avocado in a smoothie or pudding – This sounds weird but it works! Avocado gives the smoothie or pudding a smooth texture and adds healthy fats. You can even use it as a substitute for dairy.

- Unsweetened canned or pureed squash or pumpkin added to baked goods or oatmeal

- Zoodles! – I wish these had been around back when I was struggling. Spiralized zucchini or squash is now available at most grocers and can be substituted for regular spaghetti noodles or mixed in 50/50.

- Grated carrot or chopped mushrooms mixed into anything that has ground meat – Put them in taco filling, sloppy joes, and burgers.

- You can even use pureed sweet potatoes, squash, and grated carrots in brownies and cakes.

> *I will increase my veggies to* _____
> *servings per day for* _____ *weeks.*

Note: If you are starting from zero or one, you can stretch this out as long as you need to until you are getting five servings.

Pro: Try New Veggies

Now that you have started adding more veggies to your meals or snacks, let's try a new one! I didn't even know what okra, jicama, and asparagus were until I was an adult (#TrueStory). Being part of a Community Supported Agriculture program where I get local produce delivered to my door has grown my vegetable repertoire immensely. If you don't have access to a CSA, head to your grocery store or a local Farmers Market and find one thing that you have never tried before. Then hit Google or Pinterest and search for a way to prepare it that sounds good to you and test it out. If you are still scared, try something new at a restaurant instead. A few times, I've told a waiter what I was trying to do and that I was hesitant to order a new vegetable because I might not like it and would feel guilty sending it back and wasteful if I didn't eat it. I asked if anyone ordered one of these veggies while I was there could he bring me just one bite of it. I only had one tell me he couldn't do that. This is how I learned I loved beets and roasted cauliflower.

Here are a few of my favorite go-to plant-based meals:

- Chopped cauliflower that I bake and mix with tahini, spicy mustard, nutritional yeast, pumpkin seeds, and smoky balsamic vinegar

- Trader Joe's cruciferous crunch or bagged coleslaw cabbage, heated just a little bit in a big pot with tahini or Zhoug sauce, nutritional yeast, Wild Planet salmon, and juice from my bottle of jalapeno peppers

- Roasted mixed peppers with cottage cheese, oregano, and olives

- Grilled asparagus with lemon and eggs

- Roasted broccoli with pecans, lemon juice, and parmesan cheese

- Roasted Brussel sprouts with anything (olive oil, salt, and pepper). This is my absolute favorite vegetable! They are also great roasted with sliced apples, pecans, and butter.

> *I will try one new vegetable per week for one month, either at a restaurant or at home.*

Master: Veggies As Grains

When I went gluten-free, I cried for two weeks. It was much harder then because of the lack of access to gluten-free foods. It was just starting to become trendy, so people were very quick to dismiss it. Don't believe I really have an issue? Well, I'll tell you I took the most undignified test of pooing in a bucket for three days and driving "the sample" to a lab. Yeah. I went there, people, because it can be severe for some of us. Non-celiac gluten sensitivity (NCGS) is a condition characterized by intestinal and extra-intestinal symptoms related to the ingestion of gluten-containing foods in the absence of celiac disease and wheat allergy.[2]

Gluten affects more than just those diagnosed with celiac disease and one of these days the studies on gluten sensitivities and intolerance will not be glossed over and will be taken seriously. Sometimes removing certain foods from our diet can be the treatment we've been looking for, so instead of taking a pill, test out your diet. #SoapboxOver

Whether you are gluten-free or not, it's still a good idea to choose veggies over grains and think of grains as more of a complement to, rather than a staple in, a meal. When you order a dish of pasta at a restaurant, you are getting your entire day's worth of grains in one sitting, if not more. I believe one of the things that helped me become leaner at age 45 than I was at 35 is that I cut out most grains. Individual needs vary, and it may not appeal to you to limit your intake to two servings or less a day, but it does work for me. No matter what, swapping out grains for veggies every once in a while (or even once a day) won't hurt you.

Here are some examples of how I substitute veggies for grains:

- Nori (seaweed), lettuce, or collard greens – I use them to wrap my food, instead of a traditional corn, wheat, or multi-grain wrap.

- Miracle noodles or shirataki noodles – These are long white noodles from the root of the konjac yam plant. They have zero calories (how is this possible?) and are very high in glucomannan, a fiber with serious health benefits.

   Warning: These smell like seawater and will shock your nostrils the first time you open them. Drain and rinse them with hot water, and you'll be fine. They are virtually tasteless, but give you that pasta feel.

- Riced cauliflower instead of rice

- Zoodles – Zucchini or squash spiralized into noodles is a great pasta replacement.

- Peppers – I use these to hold salsa, Greek yogurt (instead of sour cream), and guacamole instead of traditional tortilla chips.

- Cauliflower, butternut squash, or kale pizza crusts – Trader Joe's has these, and they are delicious.

- Ripe bananas – Mixing these with egg and protein powder make excellent pancakes!

> *I will substitute a veggie for a grain in _____ meals per week.*

REFERENCES IN THIS CHAPTER

[1] Acta Paediatrica, Wansink, Brian

[2] https://www.ncbi.nlm.nih.gov/pmc/articles/PMC6182669/

MONTH FIVE

PRODUCTIVITY: Get Shit Done (GSD)

We can always make more money, but we can't make more time. Time is a valuable resource that can get sucked away by people, tasks, and meetings. Often it is our own inefficiencies that keep us from being most effective. I use the term GSD or Get Shit Done because when I'm in this mode, I am focused and not messing around. If you prefer the term Get Stuff Done, go for it, but it doesn't do anything for me. I get stuff done all the time. I need *emphasis*. It's only when I Get Shit Done that I am in "disturb-me-at-your-own-risk" mode, and sometimes that's right where I need to be.

Novice: Batch Tasks

Batching your tasks is a huge timesaver. People often think about batching errands, but rarely about batching their tasks. Doing all of your errands in one chunk each week in an order that saves you time and money is like saving up your project work to tackle on Mondays and Wednesdays, aka GSD times.

This one can be a game-changer. Think about it: When you are craving a cookie, you don't get out all the ingredients, make one cookie, clean up everything, and put it all away. You make an entire batch at once to save time. We can do batches with our brains too. By not switchtasking all the time not only are we protecting our minds from decision-fatigue but we are also saving time by not opening and closing various programs all day long.

For example, instead of signing into my website every time I want to add something, I save those tasks for one block per week and do them all at once. Of course, if I have a broken link or typo, I fix that immediately, but the maintenance and changes I want to make can be saved for later, so I'm not reopening my admin screen every time I have a thought. I keep a running list of what I need to add in the notes section of my recurring task for *Website Maintenance*.

Items I batch:

- Bank reconciliation and bill paying
- Client check-ins
- Social media (This helps me track my time too.)
- Email (I process twice daily.)
- Proposal follow-up

> *I will batch* _____ *tasks to save time, money, and decisions.*

Pro: GSD and Focus90

One of the best things I have done for my schedule is to designate one full or half-day every week as my *Get Shit Done Day (GSD Day)*. This is a day where I don't schedule anything. I save my most intense work for this day like writing, creating content or presentations, and preparing proposals. If you can't block an entire GSD Day, at least schedule three or four hours in a row of GSD time somewhere in your week. Fifteen minutes here and 30 minutes there won't cut it. Everyone needs a morning, afternoon, or evening (if you set your schedule and work in the evenings, not if you've been working all day in a typical nine-to-five job) to be able to focus without interruption. At a minimum, schedule one hour a day with no interruptions most days, if not every day of the week (for my corporate clients who are meeting-heavy). Decide ahead of time what your most intensive tasks are for that week and schedule yourself to work on them during your GSD time.

I created a free, community-driven program called **Focus90** that I offer once or twice a week using **Zoom** virtual conferencing. You can sign up at **www.marceyrader.com/focus90** for a session that fits into your schedule. We have our video cameras on so we can see faces but our microphones are muted so there is no disruption. I kick off each 90-minute session with a productivity tip, and we all write in the chat what we plan to get done in the next 80 or so minutes. We get to work and then when the timer goes off, we write in the chat what we were able to get done. I revisit the productivity tip and we sign off. It's always interesting to hear what people get done during the session. Most people overestimate by a third what they can get done in a set period of time. It is sometimes eye-opening to find out how long we actually spend on a task, but it's also valuable to see how much faster we can get tasks done when we keep this blocked time sacred and are really focused.

Yes, GSD time has become sort of a ritual for me. I get into GSD mode by always using one of two mugs (either my Wonder Woman or Get Shit Done mug) for drinking coffee or tea (without sugar!) and listening to a specific playlist I created on **Spotify** or the *Focus* section in **Calm.com**.

I also put my **Work Well. Play More! Do Not Disturb door hanger** on my door and often put on my noise-canceling headphones. All of these little things signal to my mind that it's GSD time!

> *I will schedule GSD time every week for _____ hours and hold it sacred.*

Master: Theme Days

Now that you have the batching of tasks down, go farther by creating theme days. When you create theme days you assign tasks to specific days of the week to create a theme. This way, your brain gets into that mode quickly, you don't have to think about what day you will do which task, and you are doing less switchtasking.

My schedule varies, so this doesn't work for me every week, and I'm not so rigid that I don't shuffle things as needed, but instead of switching from marketing to writing a presentation to working with a client and back to marketing all in one afternoon, I save up my marketing tasks for one day of the week and call that day marketing day. I batch my tasks this way to make it easier for my brain by working on one type of activity at a time.

Having one day a week that you work on marketing or if you are currently working on several projects, dividing those into different days as much as possible, can keep you from getting thoughts mixed up and will allow you to focus on one particular project. This doesn't mean that if something comes up that needs to be addressed for *Project A* on Wednesday, which is your *Project B* day, that you don't address it, but if it can wait until *Project A* day, then move it forward.

Here's an example of my themes as of the writing of this book. Because I travel and some days I might be giving a corporate workshop or conference keynote, I do shuffle things around if needed, but for the most part, I try to stick to my themes:

- **Monday** – Coach clients, online course maintenance, website maintenance

- **Tuesday** – Coach clients, marketing, social media

- **Wednesday** – Coach clients, business development/mindset/strategy work, outreach

- **Thursday** – Work on presentations, write, speaker checklist, GSD time

- **Friday** – Face-to-face meetings, administrative tasks, finances

- **Saturday** – Read blog posts and watch videos curated throughout the week

- **Sunday** – Food prep, family meeting, clothes prep, and as much screen-free time as possible

> *I knew doing similar tasks together would naturally be more efficient. What I didn't expect was how much clarity, focus, and ultimately, peace Theme Days would bring to my daily work! Deciding that Tuesday morning is content marketing creation time or that Friday is internal communications day means I spend a lot less time thinking about how I should be spending my time—and a lot less time worrying that I'm not focused on the real priorities. Choosing Theme Days has felt like a weight lifted off my shoulders!* — **Matt Bailey, President, Integr8 Research**

> **I will create Theme Days for each day of the week for those tasks that aren't urgent so I can be focused and deliberate about the topic.**

DECLUTTER: Closet

When I was younger, I thought the more clothes, the better. I bought clothes for various reasons, including out of boredom, for social interaction with girlfriends or family, and to make myself feel good. I never thought of clothes as playing a functional role unless they were for racing. I also held onto things way too long until I didn't even know what I had. What I have realized in the past couple of years is that for me, clothes lead to decision fatigue. The more I have, the more

I have to choose from to make up an outfit. This might be a game or sound like fun to you, but to me, it just causes stress. Many a morning or a time spent packing for a trip, I have stood staring into my closet, drool dribbling down my chin, eyes glazed over, trying to piece together what to wear. I like to look good, and I believe I have my own style, but the mere act of putting outfits together depletes my decision-making faculties for the rest of the day.

Mark Zuckerberg, Steve Jobs, and Matilda Kahl (Art Director for Saatchi & Saatchi)[1] are among many professionals who have decided to wear a "uniform," meaning wearing the same color or style every day of the week. This is smart because it eliminates a set of decisions they may otherwise have to spend time or energy thinking about. For those of you who get energy from choosing your clothes, this may seem incomprehensible and boring. Several of you will read this and think "what's the big deal?" I appreciate that and wish I could say the same, but for me, too many options will send me into overdrive.

I will choose a boutique any day over a department store where there are too many choices. I will shop online so I can filter like a boss and see only what I am researching. Zappos makes shoe buying amazingly fast. You can filter by color, size, style, price, and brand, and look at 25 pairs of shoes in about two minutes instead of browsing store after store at the mall. Even if you love clothes, putting together outfits, and are the one your friends call to go shopping with them to help them create styles, please read this month's habit. I promise you'll get something out of it.

Novice: Closet Edit

Routine closet edits are essential for multiple reasons. I perform mine every three to six months, and I like the KonMari method of pulling everything out and deciding if I want it or not. Here are questions to ask yourself when editing your closet:

Does it fit? If you've lost or gained weight and it's more than twenty to thirty pounds from what you are currently, get rid of it. Give items you can't wear to someone who can wear them now. Clothes don't stay in style forever and for most people, it isn't motivating to keep clothes that don't fit. If you've lost weight, don't save your baggy pants as a fallback in case you regain it—you're giving yourself an out and telling yourself subconsciously the likelihood is high you'll gain the weight back. If you've gained weight, keep no more than one thing from your previous size if you want to have something to measure yourself by. Don't continue to look longingly at a closet full of clothes you hope "someday" you'll be able to wear. They will just suck your motivation and make you feel bad about yourself. If you have a spare closet, at least move them out of the one you "shop" in every day.

Is it stained, ripped, or torn? We all have clothes that we mess around the house in, but I have a Home Depot rule. If I wouldn't feel embarrassed running out to Home Depot in the middle of a project wearing that item of clothing, then I can keep it as project clothing; otherwise, it goes in the trash.

Could someone else wear this? Do you have a sweater, jacket, or dress that you never wear that someone could be getting good use out of? What's the point of keeping something that never sees the light of day? Donate your items to a charity like Dress for Success (professional business clothes for economically-challenged women), Goodwill, or local thrift stores. I like to sell mine on thredUP (Poshmark is similar). ThredUp makes it super easy for me to send my clothes via a Clean-Out Kit. They then price accordingly and sell them on consignment on their site. I choose to get credit for items that sell and then I can buy other used items that I will wear.

Is it in style? If you're hanging onto something because it might come back in fashion, note that when it does, it probably won't be for your age group. I'm not saying that you can't wear a version of what's in style at any age, but if I would have kept the hot pink bib overalls I wore when I was sixteen, I would look a little ridiculous in them now at 45. I might wear a *version* of a bib (okay, I still wouldn't because they do nothing for your figure IMHO), but not that kind.

Would I buy this? If you wouldn't pay for it in a store today, get rid of it.

Having a friend who has excellent style or a stylist to help you edit your closet is super helpful. I have a stylist come to my house and go through my clothes. The items that no longer work for me or are out of style, she tells me to toss, sell, or donate. I am not emotionally attached to clothes, so it's not hard for me. She's also honest about things that don't fit well. It's hard for us to have an objective eye for ourselves about what looks good and having someone else give us feedback can make all the difference.

Nancy Haworth of On Task Organizing gives this helpful recommendation:

When decluttering a clothing closet, it is best to first sort your clothing by category and then by color. First, place all pants together, all sweaters together, etc. Next, sort the clothing by color within each category. At this point, you will have gathered all similar items in one place, making it easier to determine what you want to declutter. For example, you may have gathered 15 pairs of black pants together, but you only want to keep your four favorite pairs.

> **I will perform a closet edit by _____ (date).**
> **I will donate nicer items to _____.**
> **I will throw away clothes that don't fit the Home Depot rule. I will enlist _____ to help me.**

Pro: *Outfit Library*

Last year I started an outfit library, and it has greatly reduced my stare-at-the-closet-glazed-eye moments. My stylist comes to my house every quarter and helps me create an outfit library. You could do this once or twice a year instead of quarterly. You could enlist a friend with a keen eye for style or even create your outfit library by yourself if you are creative with your clothes. My stylist and I figure out five to ten outfits all the way down to the jewelry and shoes and lay them out on my bed. I take a photo and store it in Evernote in a folder marked *Fashion*. I tag them with #Speaking #Networking #Casual #Travel and use this every week when I'm picking out my clothes to wear. Several apps do this, but I keep it simple with Evernote since I use it for other things. Stylebook, for example, has you take photos of all of your items individually and then you can piece them together, track how many times you've worn an item, and create packing lists. It takes a lot of time to do the photos in the beginning, but it may be worth it for some people.

Because I get such decision fatigue from deciding what to wear, I pick out my clothes on Sunday using my Outfit Library, put five or six outfits on hangers with clothespins marking the day of the week, and hang them on hooks on the back of my door. If the weather changes or I don't feel like wearing that outfit on that particular day, I still have other entirely made up outfits to choose from. This makes it so much easier for me, and I like putting them together. If this is too much for you, I still recommend getting your clothes ready the night before. When I teach my Task Mastery course and ask how many people do clothing prep, I'm surprised to hear that more men do than women!

Even if you don't get overwhelmed with your clothing choices and you like to dress in the moment, it's still a good idea to put together a couple of outfits to have at the ready in case you need to rush out the door at some point during your week.

> *I will _____ to help me with decision-fatigue or the rush to get out the door in the morning.*

Master: *Stylist or Subscription Service*

My stylist, Michelle Scaraglino, started out being my hair-dresser, who just happened to love fashion, shopping, and dressing up other people. I like style but don't like shopping or thinking about what to wear. She started working with me and realized she could turn her passion into a business. Thankfully, she has recognized that line of genius and what a difference it can make in people's lives. I've also employed a virtual stylist, the **Technicolor Priestess, Eyenie Schultz,** to help me with my emotional connection to clothes. In the past, when I worked from home, I got into a rut and stopped seeing clothes as a representation of how I feel and the image I was portraying. Eyenie helped me by shopping for clothes that I would have never bought or worn and making me realize that I wasn't expressing myself on the outside the way I felt on the inside. I also had a session with **Shauna Van Bogart,** co-founder of the Studio for Image Professionals. Shauna upleveled me even more with finding the look that matched the image I wanted to convey and teaching me to say no to items purchased for me as gifts, which I felt terrible about giving up. She also helped me deal with a few other weird emotions I had. Now I feel like my clothes aren't just things I wear but genuinely are an expression of the image I want to portray both externally and internally.

I highly recommend working with a stylist at least once. My husband lost 30 pounds, and I gifted him a session with Susan Preston of **Geek-Adonis,** who only works with men. We met her at the mall, and she shopped with him for two hours. He became a new person overnight. He started wearing clothes that actually fit him, rather than one of his 22 oversized, black logo t-shirts and super baggy jeans. Now he walks with confidence and feels better about himself.

At the time of publishing, I am also using a clothing subscription service called **LeTote.** There are several clothes rental services like **Gwynnie Bee, Fabletics,** and **Rent the Runway.**

With LeTote, I get three items of clothing and two accessories mailed to me at home. I wear them as much as I want and send them back. I wear them right away, so I can get two bags a month because as soon as my bag is scanned at the post office, LeTote starts putting together another tote for me. I have 24 hours to swap items online before my package ships if I want something different. Since I'm in the public eye, I don't like to wear clothes I've been photographed in a second time. LeTote helps me keep my clothes fresh and, in the end, probably saves me money because I don't buy many work or dressy outfits, and I don't have to spend money on dry cleaning. They take care of that. It's also great for travel. I'll take the self-addressed stamped envelope with me and mail the clothes back from the hotel if I'm not wearing them home.

You also can use personal shopping services like **thredUP, Stitch Fix,** or **Trunk Club.** They assign you a stylist, learn what you like, and ship a box with a few items on a regular schedule. You get a set amount of time to return them, and if you don't, they assume you like them and charge your credit card. This process is great for people like me who don't want to shop.

It's silly to buy a cocktail dress or suit for a one-off occasion, so I recommend Rent the Runway. Most women don't want to wear the same dress to both our cousin's and our friend's weddings. Rent the Runway is a great solution. You choose the dress, and they send it to you in two different sizes, so you can pick the one that fits best. After the event, you ship them back in the pre-addressed garment bag included, no dry cleaning necessary. Getting dressed in high style for a night out isn't just for celebrities anymore. Since you're only renting the outfit, you can get a high-priced, glamorous dress you'd never spend the money to buy for a fraction of the price.

I've heard of people skipping fun opportunities because they didn't have anything to wear and didn't want to spend the money to buy a one-occasion outfit. How sad! This is a wonderful solution for so many problems. Subscription services also allow you to be on trend and save room in your closet.

Clothing subscriptions and stylists might seem fancy-pants (pun intended) to some of you, but I can assure you, I am not fancy. I simply can't pass up this opportunity to save myself from decisions, to have new clothes while ultimately saving money from buying them, and to feel good about myself.

> *I will invest in a style session to uplevel my clothing choices and the image I want to portray. Or I will test out a clothing subscription service or a rental for a special occasion.*

HEALTH: Sleep

Sleep is so important when it comes to our health. Our bodies rejuvenate when we sleep and sleep helps our hormones function well. Sleep is beneficial for our physical well-being and necessary for strong mental health. Let's look at how to get more and better sleep with this next set of habits.

Novice: Remove the Badge

I'm so tired. I'm so tired of the badge people wear about how little sleep they get, as if it is something to be proud of. I can't hide my eye roll. It's time to remove this badge and focus on sleep hygiene.

Before I was appropriately diagnosed with Hashimoto's Disease, I had about three years of horrible sleeping. I was maxing out at around five hours a night, having terrible middle-of-the-night insomnia with massive blood sugar swings, and spending hours staring at the ceiling with thought-rumination that was out of control. Even though I was able to function at a high level on little sleep that didn't mean it was good for me.

The **Centers for Disease Control** considers sleep deprivation an epidemic in the U.S. It affects over 33 percent of the population with over ten percent of people reporting chronic insomnia. Besides the moodiness and acting-like-a-jerk syndrome that results from a lack of sleep, Short Sleepers, i.e., those who sleep less than six hours a night, are more at risk for infection, insulin resistance, obesity, diabetes, cardiovascular disease, cancer, arthritis, hormone imbalance, and mood disorders. They also have higher levels of inflammatory proteins and C-reactive proteins in their blood, which are associated with increased heart attack risk.[2]

Chronic insomnia is associated with an elevated heart rate and core body temperature, high nighttime cortisol (the belly fat hormone), and over-activation of the hypothalamus and pituitary axis. When we sleep, our internal organs rest and recover, repair tissue, grow muscles, and synthesize protein. Hormones are released to regulate appetite control, stress, growth, and metabolism. It stands to reason then that when we don't get enough sleep, all of these processes are interrupted.

Sleep deprivation is also responsible for a significant number of the motor vehicle and machinery-related accidents every year. The National Highway Traffic Safety Administration reported that in 2017, 795 lives were claimed due to drowsy driving. In 2015, they estimate that 90,000 police-reported crashes involved drowsy drivers.[3]

And it doesn't take chronic sleep issues to put you at risk either. Even one night of insufficient sleep will lower your reaction time to levels equivalent to that of drunk driving. When I used to compete in 18- to 30-hour extreme adventure races, my teammates agreed the most dangerous part was the drive home because we were tired.

Here are some interesting sleep facts and statistics from the National Sleep Foundation:

- Did you know that children are insensitive to extreme noise levels? Keeping the house quiet during naps and bedtime actually will make it harder for them to sleep through noise later in life. As we age, our threshold for noise levels decreases.

- People who struggle with insomnia or other sleep disruptions tend to have lower pain tolerances.

- When you're awake, your brain builds up beta-amyloid proteins that are biomarkers for Alzheimer's Disease. When you sleep, your brain flushes some of them out.

- People with low Vitamin D levels are more likely to suffer from sleep apnea and complain of daytime sleepiness.

- It can take two to three weeks for sleep to adjust to an altitude of 13,200 feet or more.

- Brain scans of healthy adults who have had a good night's sleep showed they were able to regulate their desire for high-calorie foods better.

- Still not convinced about the importance of sleep? Here's another point. If you don't get enough deep sleep cycles, your serotonin levels will be lower and you will be more likely to make decisions out of fear.

Because it's so important, sleep hygiene is one of the first health behaviors I work on with private clients. I usually focus on this before nutrition and exercise because most people don't have good sleep habits. Healthy sleep increases energy, results in better decision-making, strengthens the immune system, heightens our alertness, focus, and creativity, improves our client interactions, improves our mood, and increases our libido.

When we are tired, what kinds of foods do we reach for? Not energy packed foods like cruciferous vegetables, seeds, or nuts. We reach instead for refined, sugary foods and caffeine. Reduced percentages of sleep time and REM time are associated with a higher intake of fat and carbohydrates and more intense cravings for sweet and salty foods. Our brains misinterpret our sleepiness as a need for fuel. And because we don't have the focus, impulse control, or decision-making skills due to lack of sleep, we go for poor choices to feed cravings instead of the right fuel for our bodies.

Sugar and caffeine are short-term, counterfeit energy strategies.

Lack of sleep changes our hunger hormones too, which can affect our weight and body mass index. Our satiety hormone (leptin) levels decrease, resulting in increased appetite and cravings. We have impaired glucose tolerance and insulin resistance, which explains the correlation with Type 2 Diabetes. When lower levels of insulin are released throughout the night, inflammatory proteins and blood sugar levels rise. In addition, when we don't sleep, we are awake more hours during the day but are less physically active because we are tired. Also, because the same parts of the brain control sleep and metabolism, there is a positive association between sleeping six hours or fewer, having a lower resting metabolic rate (which you want to be high to burn more calories while at rest), and consuming more calories.

Besides the physical benefits of getting enough sleep, when we sleep and dream, we process and assimilate the information we learned throughout the day. Think of dreams as what we need to do to digest information and put it to use in the same way as when we eat food, we need to digest it for it to give us energy. When we sleep, memory consolidation occurs, allowing for the formation and storage of new memories. This occurs during deep, rapid eye movement (REM) sleep. When we take sleep aids, anti-depressants, and many over the counter drugs, we don't get into this REM state.

If you snore or have obstructive sleep apnea, it's crucial you take measures to deal with this issue and see a doctor for your symptoms. The good news is that sleep apnea does not have to be a permanent condition. Losing weight, exercising, wearing a mouth guard, and going on an anti-inflammatory diet can be very helpful.

People with gluten sensitivities or who have Celiac or other autoimmune diseases that are affected by gluten may find that eliminating gluten from their diets can improve sleep. I made several changes after I was diagnosed with Hashimoto's Disease, removing gluten being the most significant change. I can't trace it solely to this, but I now sleep well 80 percent of the time for a good seven to nine hours a night. Although I already had been practicing other sleep hygiene methods for a couple of years before this change, I wasn't seeing those kinds of results before. Going gluten-free may not be the answer for you, but test it out by going on a strict gluten-free diet for a month and see if it helps. It certainly couldn't hurt.

I will become a sleep champion and will prioritize sleep over _____ in order to get the proper rest my body and brain needs.

Pro: Devices and Aids

Some of us need a little help from sleep assists to get into that dream state. We also routinely use devices that prohibit us from getting good sleep.

- Forty-three percent of polled adults say they rarely or never get a good night's sleep. Ninety-five percent of those people used a computer or phone within an hour before bed.[4]

To fall asleep more easily, it's vital that you don't stay on your computer or smartphone or stare at your big screen TV until right before your head hits the pillow and you close your eyes. Your brain needs time to wind down. Not doing this has much greater health implications than just sleeplessness.

Blue light or blue rays are emitted by TV's, computer screens, and phones and are the most melatonin-suppressive of the ray spectrum.[5] Melatonin is a hormone secreted by the pineal gland in the brain. It can affect weight by modulating the action of key metabolic hormones such as insulin, ghrelin, and leptin. Melatonin suppression has been linked to an increased risk of cancer, Type 2 Diabetes, metabolic syndrome, obesity, and heart disease, as well as impaired immune function. As we age, our natural melatonin levels decrease. Blocking blue light is very effective in reducing melatonin-suppressing effects.

Ideally, you would stop using all devices at least an hour before bed, but I'm not going to pretend that all people will do that. I don't even do that most nights! Instead, I mitigate the damage.

To help with blue rays on your computer, download the program **f.lux**. It's free software that warms up your computer display at night and adapts to the time of day based on your time zone settings.

Blue blocker or gaming glasses can be helpful and are relatively inexpensive. I put them on around eight p.m. Even artificial light can suppress melatonin, so if you have issues with sleep, it's worth putting them on as soon as the sun goes down. Embarrassed about wearing gaming glasses at night? Try weighing the benefits of getting better sleep against the cost of feeling a little silly around your family. There are a lot more people out there wearing blue-blocker glasses than you think. Get over yourself and put those babies on. But if you insist on looking good, **LadyBoss Glasses** makes some really sexy blue light protection.

Adjust your settings on your phone to go into *Nightshift* mode when the sun goes down or as I do, permanently set it to happen automatically at seven every evening. This way, I'm not staring at a bright screen the last few hours before bed. For reading in bed and to cut back on the blue rays, I use prescription strength gamer glasses and a Kindle Paperwhite turned down to a warmer hue.

Besides the fact that the light plays with your brain, what happens when you get an email late in the evening that upsets you or tells you about a new task or project you are assigned to manage? You don't have time to do anything about it, yet now it's on your mind and will probably disrupt your sleep. People, we have to stop checking email and messing around on our phones in bed. Even worse is checking social media or news feeds in bed because you can scroll through them endlessly. There is nothing to tell you that you're done and you can easily get sucked into the stories or threads of comments.

To avoid all of this mess, put your phone in airplane mode, so you're not interrupted, or better yet, don't even keep it in the bedroom or beside your bed at night. I keep my phone on until my husband gets home from work, usually between eighty thirty and nine, and then it goes right into airplane mode. I use my phone for my sleep meditation and alarm, so I do keep it beside my bed but always in airplane mode. Besides, the research surrounding EMFs (electromagnetic fields) are enough for me to turn off the phone at night when I'm not using it. I don't need EMFs near my head for eight or nine hours each night. Airplane mode, please![6]

Worried about melatonin suppression? Melatonin is a hormone that occurs naturally in tart cherries and purslane (a green leafy plant in the succulent family). If you use a supplement, take the lowest possible dose first to see if it works for you. Natural Calm Magnesium Powder has a version with melatonin that I only use when traveling across time zones. But be careful as melatonin can have a Goldilocks effect. If you take too much, it can actually keep you from falling asleep. Your body may also become dependent on it and stop creating its own melatonin. I prefer regular **Natural Calm** magnesium powder and have it every night a couple of hours before bed. As an additional benefit, if you have constipation issues, supplemental magnesium can help. I travel with the individual packets since the dry air, altitude, and air pressure on planes can constrict our organs and cause more bathroom time than we want in a hotel. Yes, it's true. It's not that you are bathroom shy when you travel, there is a physiological reason why you can't go!

- Up to half of adult men and women in the U.S. are deficient in magnesium anyway, so a small amount won't cause issues.[7] Magnesium can regulate the body's flight or fight response, and it increases the neurotransmitter GABA, which encourages relaxation. I could write an entire chapter on magnesium and its uses and benefits. When in doubt, do your own research.

While we're on the subject of relaxation, what about other um . . . medicinal aides? Marijuana significantly increases endogenous melatonin, but the research is mixed on whether or not it helps with sleep and REM cycles. Cannabidiol, or CBD (hemp) oil, has also proven useful for some people.

It did nothing for me when I took it, but it affects people differently.

If you struggle with noise sensitivity, ear plugs might help. Some people can use foam or custom-made earplugs. I don't like the feeling in my ears, so I use a noise machine or app instead. I'm a fan of white noise (haha!) . . . from fans, air conditioners, or white noise apps. After I couldn't take one more middle-of-the-night serenade from the doggie daycare and boarding kennel behind our former house, we bought an Ecotone Sound and Sleep Machine. It was a little pricey, but the sound adjusts to the volume of noise in the room and was well worth the cost.

I also use my meditation app **Calm.com** to listen to the rain, ocean waves, relaxing music like Brahm's lullaby, or exclusive soundtracks by Moby or Sigur Ros. This is helpful when I travel too. It works in airplane mode, and I can set the timer so it doesn't drain the battery if I can't plug in my phone. I also use a sleep hypnosis app from **Mindifi** that has a particular version for waking up in the middle of the night or when your bedmate is snoring. If it's the middle of the night or my husband is in bed with me and I don't want to disturb him, I use **Acoustic Sheep Sleepphones**, which look like a 1980s sweatband. They plug into your phone with a super long cord and have flat speakers that lay against your ears. They're comfortable, and I don't worry about anything falling out of my ears.

For light sensitivity, I have black-out blinds in my bedroom and don't turn on lights for middle-of-the-night bathroom trips. I also wear an eye mask because I need total darkness. I prefer the **Dream Essentials Contoured Sleep Mask**. It looks like a bra for your eyes and doesn't lie flat against your face, so it's way more comfortable than typical masks. If you take a nap during the day, it won't mess up your eye makeup or leave wrinkles and crinkles either. The Dream Essentials company sells way more fancy masks, but this is my favorite. And don't worry, men, you will not be mistaken for a woman and you will get better sleep!

Prescription Sleep Aids

I admit it. About 15 years ago, I used to be a fan of prescription sleep aids. I thought that half-drunk feeling the next morning meant that I slept hard. Being in clinical research, I decided to dig a little deeper into the safety and efficacy of these products. Since then I have never put one in my mouth. For two major sleep aids on the market, the effect of the medication is falling asleep 15 minutes faster. That's it, folks. It doesn't take much to be clinically significant. I promise, the downside to that precious 15 minutes isn't worth the upside.

Prescription sleep aids have been linked to memory impairment, loss of balance, morning hangover, dizziness, sleepwalking, sleep eating, sleep sex (as in not remembering that you had it, which you would not want to admit to your partner), depression, headache, dry mouth, anterograde amnesia, and constipation. I could go on and on. I'm not anti-drug and there may be very short-term situations where you may need sleep aids. Just remember that they interfere with the natural sleep/wake drive and can create a rebound effect leading to more insomnia later. Prescription sleep aids have also been linked to increased mortality. Are all of those risks really worth an extra 15 minutes of sleep? I don't think so.

In a different direction, you could also try lavender oil. The smell of lavender can promote relaxation and restful sleep. I use **Grow Fragrance** on my sheets before bed and travel with a lavender oil roll-on to put on my pulse points, ears, and under my nose.[8]

> *I will take the following steps with my devices and sleep aides to get better sleep: _____.*

Master: Routine

Good sleep begins the moment you wake up, and many things you do throughout the day can impact the quality of your slumber. If you have children, you know that the bedtime routine is critical. I've been at friends' houses and sat alone on a couch while they went through every step of their 90-minute sleep routine with their child. I'm not saying that you have to be that diligent, but at what age do we stop getting ourselves ready for bed? Don't we need to wind down as adults just as much as we did as children?

Creating a sleep routine at home and maintaining that routine as much as possible if you travel will help improve your sleep. If you have to, set a timer or reminder (the iPhone actually has a setting for this) to remind you when it's time to start the process. I know if I wait too long, I'm too tired and then it's a vicious cycle of procrastinating to wash my face and brush my teeth because I'm beat, but I won't go to bed until I've done it.

I say the routine starts in the morning because sometimes we sacrifice sleep for other things when we might be better off with more shut-eye. I used to wake up super early to get in a long workout, when ultimately, I would have been better off sleeping an extra 20 or 30 minutes and making my workout shorter but more intense. Note I did not say I would skip my workout! :) Daily exercise positively affects sleep; however, some people need to avoid intense exercise three to four hours before bedtime.

Wake up at your natural time whenever life allows. If you aren't sure what your natural sleep and wake time is, you can take the **Morningness-Eveningness questionnaire by the Center for Environmental Therapeutics**. Expose yourself to sunlight as much as you can first thing in the morning. Use an app that wakes you at the right time in your sleep cycle if you can keep it in airplane mode and have the discipline not to look at it before bed. In the winter, you can use a lightbox, especially if you suffer from seasonal affective disorder or SAD. A light therapy box mimics outdoor light and is best used within the first hour of waking up for about 20 or 30 minutes.[9]

Avoid or limit caffeine after about two p.m. Even if you can drink soda at dinner or coffee afterward and fall asleep that doesn't mean the caffeine isn't affecting your sleep quality. Contrary to how it's typically used, coffee is best consumed when you are relaxed, healthy, and calm. Adding a stimulant onto an already stressed and fatigued person makes you more stressed and tired and leads to a vicious cycle. Stimulants like caffeine make the adrenal glands work harder, promote more significant blood sugar swings, and can often disrupt sleep once they wear off. The same thing happens with sugar before bed. Once those stress hormones are released from your sugar crash, it disrupts your pattern.

Naps are great energy boosters, but if you have trouble falling asleep at night, avoid naps late in the afternoon or for longer than 30 minutes. I set a timer and lie down in the afternoon on days I'm feeling run down.

Okay, I'm gonna be a buzzkill now, but if you care about your sleep, avoid alcohol in the evening. Alcohol is a double agent. Many people think it helps them sleep, and it does make you feel more relaxed, but it also disrupts the deep REM sleep cycle. Once the sedative effect wears off, you're more likely to awaken during the night. This is especially true for females. This is one of the reasons why it's harder to wake up the next day after drinking. A rule of thumb from **Stanford's Sleep Center** is waiting one hour per drink before heading to bed. So if you've had three martinis in an evening, make sure you stop drinking three hours before bedtime.

Avoid heavy, spicy, or sugary meals before bed. These can give you indigestion, acid reflux, or stimulate your senses and make it harder to sleep. Personally, if I eat sugar before bed, I get nightmares, probably from the release of stress hormones when my blood sugar is trying to stabilize. Food rich in tyrosine, such as cheese, soybeans, beef, lamb, pork, fish, chicken, nuts, seeds, eggs, dairy, beans, and whole grains may keep you awake and increase energy. Test out different foods to find out what affects you. It may help to start keeping a food journal, so if you have a particularly bad night, you can refer to the journal to see what you ate and when.

On the other side of the spectrum, don't go to bed hungry. If you are hungry (truly hungry, not just craving something), then how soundly do you think you will sleep for the next eight hours? Have a light snack with protein and healthy fat.

To control blood sugar, I'll sometimes have a tablespoon of nut butter or coconut manna if I'm hungry before bed. But try not to get into the midnight snack habit. It just trains your body to wake up and need a snack.

People think about turkey and how it puts them to sleep, but turkey actually isn't the best source of tryptophan. There is more tryptophan in chicken, shrimp, and soy. The reason you fall asleep at Thanksgiving is due to the massive number of calories, mostly carbs, that you consumed. By the way, there is nothing in milk that helps you sleep. If anything, it's just a placebo effect.

Chamomile tea can be helpful for some people, but it's actually a diuretic and may cause you to wake up several times during the night to use the bathroom. Like you might do with a child, I cut off my fluids a couple of hours before bed.

Eliminate as much light as possible. Use blackout curtains or blinds, an eye mask, and cover your alarm light. I even put black electrical tape on my smoke alarm light.

Change your mattress every nine or ten years or per manufacturer recommendation. Update your pillow every one or two years.

The room temperature for an ideal sleep is between 60 and 67°F. Temps below 54° and above 75° can cause less restful sleep.

Some people swear by taking a warm bath. It's not the warm bath that causes you to be sleepy, it's actually the change in body temperature. You can take a warm bath or shower or an ice bath or cold shower and any of them will help you sleep. For several years when I was training, I took ice baths. I can't do it now because my Raynaud's Disease is too severe, but I loved it when I did it back then. It feels like torture for the first couple of minutes, but if done in the evening, it can help you sleep at night due to the rapid drop and then rise in body temperature. It also helps raise your pain tolerance and ability to withstand discomfort. If you want to give it a try, stop at a convenience store and get one or two bags of ice and put them in the tub with water up to your hips while seated. I never filled the whole tub, but just up over my legs and hips. The research showing positive effects for muscle soreness is mixed, but you still may find yourself addicted as I was.

Stick to a sleep schedule as much as possible, even on the weekends. My body is in such a routine that even if I'm out at a late show or concert and don't get in bed until one a.m., the latest I could sleep in would be seven.

If you wake up during the night and can't go back to sleep after 15 minutes, get out of bed and do something relaxing until you get tired again. Do not pick up an electronic device or start working. If I wake up, I listen to a meditation, read my Kindle Paperwhite (with blue-ray blocking glasses), or fold laundry to help me get back to sleep. If you stay in bed, you'll train your brain to stay awake.

Here's my personal sleep routine:

- I wake up naturally as often as possible (anywhere between five and six thirty a.m.).

- I exercise!

- I stop all caffeine by two p.m.

- Most nights, I do not have spicy or sugary foods in the evenings. But when it's the weekend, and I want a dessert— that's a different story. I still try not to have it too late.

- About an hour before I plan to go to sleep, I wash my face, brush my teeth, change clothes, and put on my gaming glasses.

- I read until my husband gets home or if it's a weekend, we might watch a movie.

- If Kevin is home before nine thirty, I'll stay up and talk to him but put myself to bed by ten. If he isn't going to be home, I crawl into bed around nine, sometimes even eight (!) and read.

- I turn on my sleep machine, spray my sheets with Grow lavender spray, and get a chapter of fiction or light reading in. Then I turn on a meditation or hypnosis session, put my eye mask over my eyes, and go to sleep.

Because I travel so frequently, I try to stick to this routine as much as I can on the road so my body knows what's going to happen, and I can wind down as normal.

> *I will incorporate the following habits and items into a sleep routine* _____.

REFERENCES IN THIS CHAPTER

[1] https://www.harpersbazaar.com/culture/features/a10441/why-i-wear-the-same-thing-to-work-everday/

[2] https://www.cdc.gov/sleep/index.html

[3] https://www.nhtsa.gov/risky-driving/drowsy-driving

[4] https://www.sleepfoundation.org/press-release/annual-sleep-america-poll-exploring-connections-communications-technology-use-and

[5] https://www.ncbi.nlm.nih.gov/pubmed/12533495

[6] https://techwellness.com/blogs/expertise/is-wifi-safe-distance-is-key-emf-protection

[7] https://thesleepdoctor.com/2017/11/20/magnesium-effects-sleep/

[8] https://www.ncbi.nlm.nih.gov/pmc/articles/PMC3612440/

[9] https://www.mayoclinic.org/diseases-conditions/seasonal-affective-disorder/in-depth/seasonal-affective-disorder-treatment/art-20048298

MONTH SIX

PRODUCTIVITY: Concentration

People loosely joke that they have *Attention Deficit Disorder* (ADD), but what they have are poor attention skills because they haven't trained their brains to be focused. They have developed behaviors that encourage distraction. The people who suffer from actual ADD are in a different class and may sometimes need more than behavioral change to be able to move forward. *Attention Distraction Disorder* is a disorder I made up.

Before we get into the nitty-gritty, it's essential to understand why we do the things we do, even when they are self-defeating. Human brains have two kinds of attention: involuntary and voluntary.

Involuntary attention is triggered by outside stimuli and is used for survival. It's vital if you're trying to run from an avalanche, but our brains have a hard time determining that the phone ringing, pinging, or buzzing isn't an avalanche. It still takes our mind out of focus mode. Almost all individuals have a hard time ignoring loud noises and flashing lights.

This could be dogs barking, airplane noise, or a cell phone ringing in the background.

Voluntary attention is the ability to focus on a task—like me writing this book or you reading it. While reading this book, have you put it down three times in the last fifteen minutes to check something on the computer, get something to drink, or answer the phone? Focused attention takes mental energy. It's a workout for your brain. You may run an extra five minutes or complete a few more reps when you are training your body but most people don't consider training their minds. Forcing yourself to wait five more minutes before you recheck email or committing to working for 30 minutes straight on a project or task is a workout for your brain. That's why it's hard at first.

> *Developing greater control over your attention is perhaps the single most powerful way to reshape your brain and thus your mind. You can train and strengthen your attention just like any other mental ability. —* **Rick Hansen, PhD., Buddha's Brain**

As we continuously undergo interruptions, effortful control—the part of the brain that regulates attention—declines. The more you check your messages, the more you feel the need to check them. It is indeed an addiction or compulsion and results in telepressure. It can take a long time to get over because it is a process within your brain.

Multitasking Myth

It's probably apparent when we are multitasking that we are not absorbing as much information as when we are focused, yet we still do it. Whatever is learned while multitasking is less retrievable by the brain. Tasks requiring more attention like complex exercises or numbers and formulas are more adversely affected by multitasking during the learning process.

There are two types of memory processes: *Procedural memory* is how you ride a bike or tie your shoes. *Declarative memory* is remembering what you had for dinner last night or your friend's phone number. If you are a self-professed multitasker, consider which of these processes you want in control. The part of the brain called the hippocampus manages demanding cognitive tasks and creates long-term memories. It's critical for declarative memory. When you are multitasking or distracted, the hippocampus kicks jobs down to the striatum, which handles mundane tasks. The striatum is the part of the brain that is damaged by cognitive illnesses like Parkinson's Disease, where people have trouble learning new motor skills but no problem remembering things from their pasts. When you're multitasking, the mundane part of your brain may be the one replying to the question on the conference call or writing a response in an email because the hippocampus part of the brain can't do two things at once. The striatum is the brain's autopilot. Do you want your autopilot to send your client an email?

Multitasking is not a behavior of the "super-worker." Science proves it's a sign of distraction. If a person is trying to read an email while talking on the phone, the brain is trying to perform two language tasks that have to go through the same cognitive channel. The person's mind has to go back and forth between tasks, therefore slowing it down.

- Researchers at the University of Michigan found that

productivity dropped as much as 40 percent when subjects tried to do two or more things at once. One of the study's authors asserts that quality work and multitasking are incompatible.[1]

- In a study at the **University of Minnesota**, test workers who switchtasked or multitasked took 3 to 27 percent more time to complete reading, counting, or math problems. The more difficult the interrupted task, the harder it was to get back on track.

- **A Microsoft study from the University of Illinois** found it takes the typical worker fifteen minutes to refocus on a serious mental task after an interruption such as responding to an incoming email or Instant Message. It was also easier for them to stray and browse personal websites after the pause.

- A study at **UC Irvine** reported it took 25 minutes to get back on task after an interruption!

To truly learn something, your brain has to be focused 100 percent. — *Winifred Gallagher*, **Rapt: Attention and the Focused Life**

"How is your ability to multitask?" is a popular interview question. I had a trainee tell me they lied during an interview and said it was "great," but in reality, they knew that multitasking decreased productivity, and they tried to avoid it. They thought twice about taking the job at that company after knowing that it was so important that it was an interview question. I work with a lot of Human Resources professionals and tell them that if the company job description still states multitasking as a skill requirement, change it now or look completely outdated.

Multitasking in the workplace has reached epidemic proportions. The estimated loss of productivity by multitaskers to the U.S. economy is $650 billion a year.[2]

Novice: Pomodoro Technique

Because I am easily distracted, I had to learn to work in intervals. I highly recommend interval work to give you energy breaks. Make a deal with yourself to work for 45 minutes and then give yourself five or ten minutes to get a drink or stand up and move around. We are not robots.

Everyone needs a break. Initially, I felt guilty for taking these frequent breaks. Then I realized I got so much more done because I was time capping and able to focus more effectively. My brain wasn't so tired or distracted. Your ability to focus naturally ebbs and flows throughout your day. During my first work sprint (see the GSD section from Month Five) in the morning, I can easily go 90 to 120 minutes, so I take advantage of that time to focus on my Top Task. After that, I have to go in shorter intervals as my willpower and focus declines throughout the day. You will undoubtedly take as much time as you give yourself, so cap it, focus, and do it in less time when you can.

Depending on what the task is, I sometimes use the Pomodoro or Tomato Technique. The most basic way to describe it is to set a timer for 25 minutes and work wholly focused on one thing, followed by a five-minute break. It's best if this break involves getting up, moving a little bit, and looking away from the computer. Then when the timer goes off, go through another 25-minute round. After four rounds, take an extended break of 15 or 20 minutes. If you think you won't get as much done, you're wrong. Unless you are someone who can get lost in your work or project (and I envy you!), these intervals of short focus and short breaks will make you much more efficient.

I was surprised to find that even 25 minutes of focused work is sometimes hard for me. When a thought enters my mind, or I want to click on a new link, I jot it down on a piece of paper beside me and come back to it later. When I first started with the technique, I put a tick mark on paper every time I got distracted during that round. I realized after a few weeks what my good times of day were and which behaviors quickly pulled my mind off a task.

The Pomodoro Technique also helps train you on how long a project or task will take. After estimating how many Pomodoros it would take to complete an email campaign and then realizing it took me twice as long as I estimated helped plan my next campaign. I use an app called **focus booster** that not only runs a countdown timer on my screen but also keeps track of my assigned "clients" or tasks that I'm working on. I can run a report showing how much time I worked on specific tasks each week. So now I know how much time I spent writing this book and how long it took me to create a proposal, for instance. It also keeps track of money earned if I assign a dollar value to each client.

The 25-minute time limit not only works if you are trying to stay focused but also keeps you from staying on other tasks too long (I'm talking to you, Facebook and Twitter!) and works as a reward to complete even the tasks that you don't like.

Items I typically Pomodoro include:
- Housework
- Food prep for the week
- Social Media
- Email
- Internet Surfing
- Writing

47 percent of new focus booster users find they always underestimate how long it will take them to complete a task, but after a week of using the app that number drops to nine percent. The Pomodoro technique is especially useful for people working independently or remotely as it helps you to plan your day in a way that makes progress achievable (you only add to your list what is possible in the time you have), then the timer keeps you motivated and breaks keep you fresh. At the end of the day you feel a great sense of accomplishment when you see you have crossed everything off your list. — *Alice Coleman, Founder, focus booster*

I will Pomodoro these tasks for one week to determine how long I take on a task:

_____.

I will Pomodoro these tasks because I get sucked in and don't want to take a mental break:

_____.

> *I will Pomodoro these tasks because I don't want to do them and procrastinate: _____.*

Pro: Squirrel Blockers

I call these Squirrel Blockers after **Dug the Dog** in the movie *Up* and his constant distraction when he sees a squirrel. We have these squirrels all day, and sometimes we need to save ourselves from ourselves by installing a system or tool to prevent us from getting distracted by the interruptions. I'm not smarter than the creators of Google, Amazon, LinkedIn, or other sites I can get sucked into. I need a firewall against procrastination.

There are several programs and apps to help us focus. **RescueTime** allows the blocking out of distracting websites during focus time. You can categorize websites and applications from very distracting to very productive and see at the end of the day or week how productive you were in managing distractions. Set goals and work to stay within those parameters every day. RescueTime is free for the basic service, but the paid premium is worth the investment.

Freedom lets you schedule blocks of time to prohibit opening all sites or only allowing a few specific sites to open. If you absolutely must go back online, you have to restart your computer. I used Freedom to keep me focused on writing this book. I also have a block from eight p.m. to nine a.m. every day from social media and email (because email is never my Top Task) and all day on Sunday. One feature that Freedom offers and other similar apps don't is that it works across all devices. You can't cheat and get on your phone when you've blocked yourself on your laptop, for example. This is one of the ways I save myself from myself.

ChromeNanny lets you block sites at specific times of the day. If you want to make sure you don't check Facebook or Twitter at work, set it up to prevent access during your workday.

Facebook News Feed Eradicator is an extension that replaces your newsfeed with an inspiring quote.

Successful and efficient people aren't always more disciplined; they just set themselves up better and prepare for success. Making it difficult to continue with a behavior, or even to have to think twice about that behavior, can be enough for behavioral change.

> *I will install* _____ *to save myself from myself.*

Master: Circadian Rhythm Schedule

If you really want to geek out on learning when you are most productive, you can take the **Morningness-Eveningness questionnaire by the Center for Environmental Therapeutics**. It's a 19-question tool on daily sleep-wake habits that gives you a "circadian rhythm type." It takes about five to ten minutes and returns a report that tells you your estimated time of melatonin onset and natural bedtime.

I'm a definite morning person and do not apologize for it

when I want to go to bed early. It's also why I don't give up my early mornings for networking or business events (it better be good) or even to coach clients. I get energy from my clients and can't help but be engaged, so I use my mornings to get my Top Tasks done because I know the later it gets, the more likely I will be to procrastinate.

> *I will complete the Morningness-Eveningness questionnaire and test one week (one month is ideal) to go to bed and wake up according to my estimated natural rhythms and perform focused work at my most productive times.*

DECLUTTER: Media FOMO

Fear of Missing Out is pervasive throughout our society. If our friend asks us about the latest current event and we aren't aware, we immediately feel behind the times. If we haven't binge-watched the newest season of *Ozark*, we aren't cool. If we don't have a presence on social media, we must not exist.

I heard the term JOMO—Joy Of Missing Out—and have adopted it for my own life, though I actually prefer JOOO—Joy of Opting Out—since I'm not actually *missing out* on anything. I cannot know everything around the world that is going on, be up to date on all the latest shows, or even possibly care about what celebrity has done the most recent ridiculous thing on social media. And guess what? I am still relevant. I am current with the people I care about and will get any news I don't see on social media on *NPR*, The Daily Podcast, or from my husband who spends a substantial amount of time on *Reddit*.

We used to (only about 20 years ago!) not know every single activity someone did, but with social media, we constantly see the posts of parties attended and vacations taken. People under 40 can't even imagine a time when the news wasn't 24/7, and it's becoming harder and harder to decipher a reputable news source. (Hint: it's not Facebook or Twitter, people.)

A study in *Psychology Today* reported that FOMO is associated with fatigue, stress, sleep problems, and psychosomatic symptoms. It had nothing to do with personality. Even introverts experience FOMO. When testing to see if FOMO was directly related to social media, they discovered that whether it was seen online or heard about via a friend, FOMO existed at the same rate.

Social Media, sports, and news channels can easily become a time suck if you don't time cap or limit the number of days you check your accounts. The platforms are built to keep you on them using the same psychology of endless feeds without stopping points just like the windowless rooms without clocks in casinos. If you don't feel like you have FOMO, perform the habits below for one month and then revert back if you want to.

Why is this in the decluttering section? Because it's about decluttering your mind, not just your environment, and a lot of input we allow would constitute clutter.

Novice: News

In an age of 24/7 news, I can sit at only one table in my

business club and not have to look at a TV screen while I eat my lunch. It's challenging to get away from all of the bad things going on in the world. It's our own fault. When the **City Reporter** conducted an experiment to test negative versus positive news angles, the audience decreased by two-thirds when they increased the number of positive stories. Even minor changes like focusing on traffic running smoothly despite bad weather turned readers away.

News hasn't gotten more negative than in the past, we are just exposing ourselves to it more and finding out about it much sooner. This exposure can lead to disaster fatigue, making us less concerned and more apathetic about whatever the current crisis is.[3]

It can also lead to physiological, mental, and emotional symptoms in some people without them realizing that's the source of anxiety. I have significantly limited my news, not because I want to be ignorant but because the negativity I was hearing every day started to affect me so much that during one long news cycle, I developed unexplained symptoms that made me think I was developing another autoimmune disease. I had multiple tests run and realized later in a lightbulb moment crying unexpectedly in a coffee shop that I was being triggered by the current events of the time. The stress symptoms were so real I thought I was sick. It took time for me to make the connection. I was embarrassed and confused that I was having this reaction, but it wasn't intentional. I wrote a post about it at **www.marceyrader.com/metoo-made-me-think-i-was-ill.**

- In a **study done at the University of Pennsylvania,** they found that watching three minutes of negative news stories before ten a.m. resulted in a *27 percent greater likelihood* of feelings of unhappiness six to eight hours later!

Don't choose to be ignorant and dismiss news altogether. It's important to be informed. But do take a news "fast"—where you don't look at news for a specific period of time—say 24 hours—occasionally or when you start to feel stressed.

- Twitter removed *70 million fraudulent accounts in just two months* in 2018, Facebook removed *583 million fake accounts in three months* in 2018, and MIT reported that lies are 70 percent more likely than facts to be retweeted.[4] If you do nothing else, please, for the love of mint chocolate chip ice cream, stop using Facebook, Twitter, and other similar forums as your main news sources.

There are three options this month. Choose one, two, or all.

> *I will be intentional about how I get my news. For one week this month, I will take a news fast and see how it affects me.*

> *I will not succumb to the clickbait and click links posing as news stories from any social media channel and will only get news from reputable news channels.*

> *I will limit news exposure to _____ minutes per day.*

Pro: Podcasts

I am a big fan of listening to podcasts and audiobooks in the background when I'm running, driving, cleaning, taking a walk, or cooking. I use the **Downcast** app and subscribe to no more than three podcasts at a time. I typically have another one to three just so I can get an idea of the podcast style of the ones I am being interviewed for, but I tend not to keep them on my feed. My personality is that I feel overwhelmed or behind when I can't listen and they pile up. I used to subscribe to six to ten, and I would feel like a podcast failure seeing how many new ones I hadn't listened to. Those badges just called to me letting me know what a failure I was. Keeping it to two or three also makes me intentional about what I listen to and which podcasters I follow.

Why do I want to subscribe to fewer? Because I found that I was continually inputting without outputting. If I'm always listening to information going in, I'm not giving myself white space to think and get something out. It became so habitual to always have something being transmitted through my ears or eyeballs that I wasn't even respecting my own ability to think and create. Now, when I'm out of podcasts or don't have an audiobook to listen to, the rest of that day I don't let myself search for something new. I listen to music or enjoy the silence.

If you subscribe to podcasts that are just "meh" or if you get overwhelmed like I do, for the love of kittens, unsubscribe! There are a few top-rated podcasts I used to listen to because friends, my husband, or someone famous in my field did, but in the end, I need more time in my day for white space to think more than I need to have information continuing to come in.

You may not listen to a lot of podcasts or care that there are 15 you haven't heard. If so, it's still good to reevaluate if what you have is continuing to give you value and you look forward to listening to them. There are so many out there, "meh" isn't even an option. Subscribe to the ones you would truly miss if they stopped podcasting.

If you don't listen to any, you can exchange podcasts with movies or series and whittle down your Netflix, Prime, or Hulu queue.

> *I will review my podcasts, remove all of them that are "meh," and focus on the ones that bring joy, interest, or learning into my life.*

Master: *Social Media*

I know this is where I may lose some of you, but stick with me for a month. Like many business owners, I consider much of social media a time suck. There are so many social media channels I can't even keep up with them all. When I started my company, I narrowed it down to five channels: YouTube, Google+, Facebook, Twitter, and LinkedIn. In January 2019, I went to LinkedIn only, and it has been absolutely fantastic. I have not lost any business, nor have I felt like I was missing out on the people I genuinely care about. Instead, I visit them, call (yes, words and talking!), text, or email. Not spending so much time on social media has opened me up to so many other things to devote my energy to. I even wrote about my experience on LinkedIn—**https://www.linkedin.com/pulse/what-happened-when-i-switched-linkedin-only-marcey-rader/**

A couple of my clients who had FOMO would sleep with their phone and check Facebook before they even got out of bed in the morning. If you don't feel you have a problem with social media and it *truly brings you joy*, don't worry about it, but most of my clients say they don't want to spend as much time on it as they do.

A study in the *Journal of Social & Clinical Psychology* found that there is indeed a causal link between social media and adverse effects on well-being to include depression and loneliness. People who used less had better outcomes. (Note: they didn't require anyone to completely eliminate it.)[5]

Social media can lead to more negative emotions following use—jealousy, social tension, isolation, and depression. People are putting their best foot forward in social media, so you don't see the bumps in their roads. If social media overwhelms you and you're using it for personal use only, it might be worth it to delete that account and set up a new one. Be choosier about those you allow into your circle or list of friends. Before I had my business, I used a fake name so I couldn't be found. If the people or companies you like don't add any value, then don't waste good eyeball strength reading them. I currently have no personal accounts except LinkedIn, and I don't feel like I miss out.

When I did have a personal account for Facebook, I had "friending" rules (see my mindmap on page 36) that included:

- Over 18 years old

- No coworkers or business peers unless I would have them over for dinner

- Friends and family I would have over to dinner if they were in town (This includes family because I have a big, extended family.)

- People who didn't overshare private issues (I had to unfriend family members who do not know the meaning of privacy. I didn't know whether to feel sorry or embarrassed for them.)

- Business Pages of the people I supported and was interested in their products or services

- A maximum of 20 people on Facebook (I didn't want to invest any more time than that required. It made me think carefully about whether I just wanted to be a voyeur in their lives or I genuinely cared about them.)

I also forced myself to wait to post instead of doing it at the moment. When I'm visiting the icy waterfalls of Huatulco, I need to be taking it in, not posting about it. I can post in the hotel room (or on the plane ride home). When I was in Dubai, I took photos all week and then waited to make a photo spread when I got back. Why spend my time in such an exotic place posting online instead of seeing the sites? Last, if I did any actual thinking about how I would post it on social, rather than just enjoying the moment, I made myself pause. I want to be doing and acting for myself, not for an audience.

I established these rules, so it was easy for me to explain why I clicked ignore when someone asked to friend me. I would check social media once per week for no more than 25 minutes and quickly scan my business accounts a maximum of five minutes per day. I set a Pomodoro to time cap it so I didn't get sucked in. This also included any links or videos that I visited while on that channel.

Set guidelines for yourself on how many social media platforms you will join, how often you will visit them, and how much time you will spend on each.

> *I will create guidelines around social media that work for me that will include removing "friends" or "connections" that don't fit specific criteria to unclutter my feed and make room for real friends.*

> *I will limit my time to ____ minutes, _____ days of the week, remove the app from my phone (the horror!), and be intentional about when I am using it.*

HEALTH: Exercise

Earlier in the book, I shared my story about my relationship with exercise, which cycled back and forth between healthy and unhealthy. Now, I feel like I'm in a very healthy mindset and treat my body with respect. I love to exercise. Yes, you guessed it. To me, it's like brushing my teeth. When people ask if I still work out on vacation, I ask them if they always brush their teeth, take a shower, or drink water even though they are on vacation. Of course I do because:

- It's a habit, and it's harder to restart a practice than to start a brand new one.

- My body doesn't know it's on vacation. It doesn't know what day of the week it is. It only knows that it responds well and feels better when I move.

- Most of my vacations are active anyway, so while it may not be my typical routine, I'm still getting a lot of exercise.

But I don't always feel like exercising. Ask me to go for a run after work and it won't happen. Plan to ride my bike in the middle of the day? Only when I have set myself up to do that in advance. My morning routine involves exercise no matter what because for me, the longer I go, the more things I will find to keep me from getting it done. Just like I would put my oxygen mask on first on the plane, I will do this for myself every morning before I give one minute to anything else.

I have two degrees in Exercise Science and Nutrition plus multiple certifications through the National Academy of Sports Medicine and the Institute of Integrative Nutrition. However, even I eliminate my decision-fatigue and purchase programs so I don't have to think about my workout. I outsource that to an app or, in the past, to a coach. Now, before the non-exercisers skip to the next chapter, stick with me here and commit to the Novice habit this month.

Novice: Just 5, 7, 10 by 10® or 25 in 25®

Good news! There are some things in life where even just a little can make a big impact. If you do it right, exercise is one of them. You do not have to change your clothes (okay, ladies, you may need a sports bra to protect your girls), drive to a gym, or even drip with sweat to benefit. You don't need equipment, a membership, or a full hour. Anyone can exercise even with a fully-packed schedule.

Here's what I want you to do: commit to one of these four behaviors, mix them up, or spread this habit out over four months and build it that way.

Just five minutes

Commit to doing a five-minute exercise routine every day of the week. Yes, every day because there is no need to take a rest day when you're only doing five minutes. Download the **Sworkit** app, which is all exercises that can be done using bodyweight only (no equipment necessary) and can be used for cardio, strength, yoga, or stretching. This is a fabulous app voted #1 by the American College of Sports Medicine and University of Florida. You can choose videos lasting from 5 to 60 minutes, and they guide you through each movement. I've used this in hotels and parking lots when I've traveled. One of my clients had a five-minute Movement Opportunity Sworkit every morning. **Zuzka Light** also has five-minute workouts, and I have several on a YouTube playlist I created years ago. They're oldies but goodies.

Seven-minute workout

The American College of Sports Medicine released a study in 2013 showing that you can get maximum results with minimal time investment in a seven-minute workout.[6] The only thing you need is a sturdy chair or bench to be efficient in decreasing body fat, improving insulin sensitivity, and improving cardiovascular and muscular fitness. You work out at a higher intensity and hit every body part within a short time. And guess what? There's even an app for that—https://well.blogs.nytimes.com/2014/10/24/for-a-7-minute-workout-download-our-new-app/

Want a greater challenge? Try the Advanced 7-minute workout that involves free weights. https://well.blogs.nytimes.com/2014/10/24/the-advanced-7-minute-workout/

10 by 10®

I created two challenges that people can follow on **Coach.Me**. The **10 by 10®** is ten minutes of exercise every day before ten a.m. Why? Because doing it in the morning is a keystone habit, sets us up for healthy behaviors the rest of the day, and we're more likely to do it if we get it in by then. Note that I don't work with Coach.Me anymore, so I won't be commenting on your progress, but seeing that streak and doing the check-ins can be helpful. I don't care what you choose for those ten minutes, as long as it's exercise. I also provide some videos for bodyweight workouts you can do in a small space at home or while traveling. https://www.coach.me/plans/255-10-by-10-exercise-challenge

25 in 25®

The **25 in 25® challenge** I started about 16 years ago with my family. We do this every December, but you could do it any time of year. The full story is here: **https://www.marceyrader. com/25-25-exercise-challenge/**. Exercise 25 minutes every day for 25 days. The reason why we did this in December is that it tends to be the busiest month for most people and good habits fall to the wayside or are waiting to be created in January. I have heard from several people that this started a life-changing path for them. If they were able to do it in December, they could do it any time of year. **https://www.coach. me/plans/216-25-in-25-december-exercise-challenge**

> *As an entrepreneur, I struggled with sticking to an exercise routine for years because I felt that I needed to spend all my time building the business. My weight was the highest it had ever been the months following the writing and publishing of my first book. After joining Marcey's yearly exercise challenge, I worked out every day in December. I loved the routine and wanted to continue. I realized that I was actually **more** productive immediately following a workout. I was the most creative after exercising, which decreased the amount of time it took to write and finish new blog posts and offerings. Now, my mindset has completely changed due to Marcey's 25 in 25®️ program. Instead of feeling like exercising is just one more thing on my To Do list, I consider it a prerequisite to starting my work day . . . just like brushing my teeth after getting out of bed! It's a non-negotiable. — Sylvia Inks, SMI Financial Coaching*

I will do _____ minutes of exercise every day by using this method: _____.

Pro: *Do What You Aren't Doing*

If you started with the Novice habit, you are now intention-ally moving. If you are already an exerciser, it's now time to spend a month doing something new. Our bodies and brains get used to the activities that we routinely do, and I want you to mix it up! Most people do not have well-rounded fitness programs where they are focusing on cardiovascular health, muscular strength, agility, flexibility, and balance. We do what we like and ultimately become unbalanced. Also, as we age, some activities are even more essential to incorporate, like balance work.

Here's how my fitness regime has changed through my life:

- Teens – softball, basketball, track, and volleyball
- Early 20s – group exercise instruction and yoga
- Mid-Late 20s – running marathons, yoga, and strength training
- 30s – triathlon, ultra-running, ultra-mountain biking, and adventure racing
- 40s – running (less than 45 minutes), mountain biking, strength training, yoga, jumping rope, dance, and fitness classes

Basically, I beat myself up in my thirties and am spending my forties focusing on health and longevity. I started doing more agility work (quick, multi-directional movements) because it's going to help me prevent falls as I age. I take choreographed classes with steps I have to listen to and learn to improve my memory and coordination. These are not my favorite things to do, yet I do them because I have the endgame in mind of being strong and high-functioning well into my older age and waiting twenty to thirty years down the road to start working on this will not set me up for success.

Wait! I thought we were only supposed to do what we enjoy? Yes, you are. And I don't dislike these acts, they just aren't *my favorite* things to do. They're challenging and that's the point. Zoning out on a steady-state run or bike ride every day of the week wouldn't be doing me any favors.

Your challenge? Add something you aren't already doing. If you don't do any flexibility work, like stretching or foam-rolling, add in one to three minutes a day or an entire exercise program a week (example: one of your 10 by 10® sessions can be a foam rolling and stretching session). If you don't do any balance work, do all your standing strength training moves on one leg (example: do your shoulder presses on one leg or a balance disc). If you lack coordination, take a movement or dance class.

I don't care how much you incorporate at this point, but change it up and do something different or add a component you aren't doing now.

> *I will add _____ to my movement routine. I will do this _____ times per week for _____ minutes.*

Master: *Coach, Class, or Race*

Your challenge this month is to sign up for a class you haven't tried before, a race if you are new to the sport, or hire a personal trainer or coach, even if it's only for one session. It's crucial for us to think outside the box. Now I want you to *move* outside the box.

Taking a new class can be fun, intimidating, motivating, inspiring, and maybe it will even surprise you with a new challenge that you enjoy! If you're nervous, sign up with a friend. If you don't have a lot of money, use a Groupon or Living Social coupon and find a free or cheap introductory offer. I did this with hoop dancing years ago and became hooked (or hooped?). If you are already a group fitness junkie, sign up for a class that you wouldn't usually take, even if it's just one time.

Sign up for a race, whether it's a 5K, cyclocross, or three-legged potato sack. I'll even let you sign up for the Boerne, Texas .5K race **https://runsignup.com/Race/TX/ Boerne/BoernePoint5k**. Whether it's to challenge yourself or have fun, do a race if that's something new for you.

Hire a *certified* personal trainer or *certified* coach to help you get across that plateau, get to that next level, or show you proper technique. It would be even better if the coach or trainer had a degree in Exercise Science. If you feel stuck in a rut or you aren't sure what you are doing is the correct form, hire a trainer at a gym, sports facility, or even online. If you are already an avid exerciser, invest in a coaching program that helps you target a specific goal that challenges you.

I went crazy and developed a Big Hairy Audacious Goal to help me unlock why adopting new behaviors and chucking old ones was so tricky for my personal coaching clients. It had to be big if I wanted to understand their pain, resistance, fatigue, as well as incremental victories. At age 60, I will climb the highest

mountain in the contiguous United States: Mt. Rainier. I chose a goal that had a spiritual motivation (my mother's ashes are on the flanks), an intellectual challenge (glacial climbing techniques), and a whopper of a physical feat for someone who never really played sports. I'm a low structure person. I knew I needed a trainer to push me, plan workouts, teach me, and hold me accountable for showing up, working hard, and sticking to a strict muscle-building nutritional regimen. I'm happy to say that five months in I am the strongest and leanest I've ever been, as shown by body scans every six weeks. I've mastered my own internal mountain of doubt with purpose and persever-ance. The actual summit of Rainier? That'll be a piece of cake.
— Janet Boudreau, Executive Chair, Vistage International

If you are comfortable with what you are doing, that's great. You can go back to comfy and cozy next month. This month, I want you to challenge yourself for 30 days and do something new.

I will take _____ *class.*

I will sign up for _____ *race or challenge.*

I will invest in a coach to improve my _____ *.*

REFERENCES IN THIS CHAPTER

[1] https://www.apa.org/pubs/journals/xhp/index

[2] https://frontapp.com/blog/2018/07/20/how-much-time-are-you-spending-on-email/

[3] https://www.cnn.com/2018/06/01/health/bad-news-bad-health/index.html

[4] https://www.inc.com/magazine/201905/tom-foster/russian-trolls-facebook-social-media-attacks-brands-hoax-fake-disinformation.html?cid=hmsub2

[5] https://guilfordjournals.com/doi/10.1521/jscp.2018.37.10.751

[6] https://journals.lww.com/acsm-healthfitness/Fulltext/2013/05000/HIGH_INTENSITY_CIRCUIT_TRAINING_USING_BODY_WEIGHT_.5.aspx

MONTH SEVEN

PRODUCTIVITY: Taskicizing

We all have *To-Do* lists and while some may resist the list, when they do, they are more likely to forget what it is that needs to be done. It is not a point of pride in my life to keep everything in my head. I already have enough swirling around in my brain space. Anything I can remove to make room for new information is better for me. I listicize everything.

You can choose to use paper and pen or create an electronic list. It doesn't matter as long as it works for you. Most people use a hybrid of electronic lists for recurring tasks and paper lists for things that need to be done that day or need jotting down quickly. I use both. I have Google Tasks on my phone and laptop because it works across devices. I keep a paper notebook beside my keyboard for quick thoughts I want to jot down. I also have a whiteboard with goals, priorities, and other relevant information for the week, month, and year.

Before we jump into the logistics of tasking, I want you to thinkitate on this fundamental concept: *It doesn't matter how many tasks you complete if the right tasks aren't being achieved.* You've marked off everything on your list today. So what? Did three of those even matter? Were they just busywork? More is not always more. More is sometimes waste.

Novice: Task from Email

First, to organize your list, we start with your inbox, which is the last place to have a task list. It's hard to keep in priority order and there may be multiple tasks with multiple dates within one email. There's also the time wasted rereading that email, letting your eyeballs scan over it, or clicking through it three times a day (remember the OHIO method and Only Handle It Once from Month Three). Instead, pull out the tasks within the email and enter them into your task list or simply save the email as a task.

In Outlook,
- create a **Quick Step** called **Task**
- create a **Task with attachment**
- either *Delete message, Archive message* into a specific folder, or (if you like to put your emails in different folders) *Always ask for folder*

You only need to set up this *Quick Step* one time. Then when you have an email that is a task or you need to get back to it later, right click the email, click *Quick Step, Tasks,* and when the window pops up, assign a date to it. I keep it simple and recommend only adding a start or due date (think of it as the day you will *do* it) and changing the subject line if the nature of the task that is within the email is not apparent. Then, you have the full email within the task if you need it, and it automatically moves out of your inbox. Categorize your task list by date so you can see which tasks are a priority. Change your view settings in your inbox and calendar screens to also see your Task list.

For Gmail
- Assign emails to tasks in your menu bar by clicking **More** > **Add to Tasks**
- Archive email because the link is now automatically in your Task list, which also shows up in your calendar and email view (if you check the box in your settings)

One advantage of an electronic list is documenting repeated tasks. For example, I work on my course on Mondays. If I check it off my task list today, it automatically moves forward to next Monday because I've marked it as repeating.

Ideas for recurring tasks that aren't efficient to keep entering into a list every time you do them may include:

- Completing timesheets and expense reports
- Recurring project deadlines
- Housework or chores
- Paying quarterly taxes

Some things that I recur on my task list include:

- Writing
- LinkedIn (Yes, it's a task, not a default go-to when I want to procrastinate.)
- Prospect outreach
- Weekly Priorities

If you're a paper person, you may not need to have an electronic task list. If paper works for you, stick with it. Something as simple as writing your tasks on an index card every day can be gratifying. Cross off tasks and then throw it away when you are finished. However, it is ineffective to task your *emails* on paper. You can have a hybrid system and task your emails electronically and your daily to-dos on paper.

One disadvantage of a paper list is that you can't share all the information with a Virtual Assistant, family member, or colleague. I have a minimal hybrid system where my stream-of-consciousness thoughts go on a piece of paper beside me at my desk. I don't interrupt what I'm doing to put it on my e-list, which would be a distraction. These thoughts are typically taken care of that day, but if not, they go on my electronic list.

Ideas to listicize:

- Travel checklist (I keep this in Evernote and duplicate the list each time for different trips.)
- Shopping staples
- Items you need or want for the home
- Places you want to visit
- Questions to ask your doctor
- Holiday or gift list (Amazon wish lists are great for this.)
- All the health and productivity behaviors you want to adopt!

> *I will task from email to move the email out of my inbox and be able to Only Handle It Once!*

Pro: Top Three ABCDE

It doesn't matter how many boxes are checked if those boxes don't matter. Being busy and achieving the most tasks in one day doesn't make you a superstar. Knowing how to prioritize those tasks appropriately is the way to get to the top. Do you think Tony Robbins, Oprah Winfrey, Dave Ramsey, and Sara Blakely are just looking to check boxes all day? They didn't get where they are by getting the most things done. They got where they are by focusing on what's important.

I call this the *Top Three Method.* On the last day of the quarter, I look at my next 90 days to determine my *Top Three Priorities* for the next quarter. On the last day of each month, I jot down my *Top Three Priorities* for the next month. On my last day of the work week, I decide my *Top Three Priorities* for the next week. I write all of these on a giant whiteboard in my office, where I also capture my profit and loss, pipeline, habits I'm working on, and at least one fun thing I'm going to do that week. This helps me determine what's essential for me to work on without any question and makes me intentional about what's important.

Why only three? We really can't have more than three top priorities and arguably, there is only one priority at a time— whatever it is you are doing at that moment. However, our brains can remember things in three's, and most people shudder at thinking of only one priority for an entire 30 days or even for a week. If you have monthly or weekly meetings with your manager, ask them to share what they think your *Top Three Priorities* for the week should be. You may find that you have prioritized something that they don't consider necessary. Asking also helps to prevent procrastination because even your boss didn't include "answer all your email" as one of the *Top Three Priorities* for the week. Sometimes asking if a particular email is a Top Task may cause your manager to rethink all their urgent requests via email and their concern that you respond within minutes.

Why the month, week, or evening before? It's better to slide into your next sprint knowing what needs to be done and to determine this outside of the moment of urgency. Each evening during my transition from work mode to personal mode, I schedule my *Top Three Tasks* for the next day. I recommend this over doing it in the morning because you will end your day knowing exactly what you need to do tomorrow and won't just choose what you want to do in the moment. You also can go into your evening knowing the plan and feeling at ease. Consider the timing of those *Top Three Tasks* according to your energy levels and schedule for the day. As often as possible, abide by Brian Tracy's rule to **Eat That Frog** in his book named the same. I do my most important task (the one I will most likely avoid) first or at a time that I know I will have uninterrupted focus time. If I'm going to be working during a layover or while waiting for a client, I'll do things that I can quickly cross off my list with the minimal focus required. If it's writing or creating, I know I will need completely silent, non-distracted time, like a **Focus90** session, and will wait until I have a chunk of that available.

Causes of procrastination can be not liking the task, fear of doing a lousy job, fear of doing a good job (and getting rewarded with more work), or underestimating the time it takes to do it. Procrastination can also be selfish. If someone is expecting something, you might unconsciously wield your control by withholding what they need. If there is something you find is a common task that doesn't get done, evaluate and resolve the why.

You may have heard about the *Eisenhower Method for Priority Order*. It separates tasks into four quadrants:

- **Urgent and Important** – These tasks must be taken care of immediately. Either there is a crisis or you have procrastinated too long and it needs to be done now.

- **Urgent, but Not Important** – These are tasks that need to be done quickly and are associated or assigned by someone else or tasks where other people are waiting for you and you can't be the bottleneck.

- **Not Urgent, but Important** – These tasks help you move toward your goals and should be scheduled appropriately. If, however, you procrastinate, they can quickly move to Urgent and Important.

- **Neither Important nor Urgent** – These tasks can be sent to the bottom of the list. These are things that are "nice to have" or can be done during a light day during the week. They are activities that are distractions and probably can be discarded all together.

Think of your tasks regarding whether they are urgent or important. If they are both, then it will be obvious which belong in your top three and need your attention, even if it means shutting down your email and entirely focusing.

ABC Delegate Eliminate

But I have more than three tasks! Of course, you do! The important thing is the priority order of those tasks and to look at your day with these questions in mind:

If these three things don't get done, there could be a negative impact possibly affecting the rest of my week or other scheduled tasks.

If I were to go on vacation tomorrow, what would need to get done today so I can unplug?

If I only had 45 minutes of battery left on my device, what would I need to focus on?

When looking at all your tasks, identify and label your top three as Task A, Task B, and Task C. Then see if there are any others you can D (delegate) and/or E (eliminate).

D – Delegate those tasks that you can. If you have direct reports or an assistant, give them the skills, knowledge, and tools to take over that task and then trust them with it. If it's a home task, can you outsource to **TaskRabbit** or hire a professional?

E – Eliminate other tasks. Skim through your tasks every day and determine if there is anything you can eliminate. "Nice to have" tasks mean nothing and typically don't add value. If your client wouldn't pay you your hourly wage for the two hours you spend formatting that spreadsheet perfectly, stop doing it. If you are thinking of creating a report that no one asked for but you think might be helpful and would take you 30 minutes, eliminate it.

Are there any tasks you repeatedly push forward to the next day over and over again? If so, they probably don't need to be done. Chuck 'em. It's good practice to evaluate your tasks now and then to determine if they are even still a priority.

Being focused and able to concentrate on a task only works if you can discriminate. It doesn't do any good to be focused if you are spending that time on irrelevant or "outside your line of genius" tasks.

Discriminate to concentrate:
Discriminate first, then get focused.

We shouldn't discriminate against hairless cats, planned communities, or cauliflower, but we should discriminate against our D and E tasks.

Before implementing ABC Delegate Eliminate and identifying three essential items the night before, I dealt every day with a mile long list that seemed like it never got smaller. And my afternoon was spent wallowing in "I will never make progress on this list and it will be moved to tomorrow which will likely be worse. Is there anything I can check off to call this day any part of success?" Of course, I could only work on quick things with that perspective and so it became self-fulfilling. I went home most days discouraged and rarely felt the feeling of accomplishment I was looking for. After about two weeks of doing ABC almost every day, I have checked more off and ended more days feeling accomplished than in months prior. Today, I'm going home before 4pm (typically 5:30 or later). I already checked off some of tomorrow's list because my top three were done by 2:30pm. Plus I know (because I worked the list last night) that there's nothing there more important or pressing than what has already been accomplished today. My wife and daughters will be surprised to see me home early for a change. I'm grateful for the time to Play More! — Eric Syfrett, Pastor and Financial Consultant

> **I will prioritize using the Top Three Method and for the priorities or tasks I have left, I will first determine if I can Delegate or Eliminate them.**

Master: Task Management System

When you are working solo, a simple task management system or To-Do list can work. If you are working with even one person or you are a company that has conversations and check-ins via email, start using a project management system like **Asana, Basecamp, Microsoft Teams,** or **Trello.** There are so many to choose from you are bound to find one that works well for you. I have one full-time employee and several contractors and do everything in Asana. My assistant and I exchange an average of one email per month. All tasks and communication are done via Asana, so we can prioritize, assign dates, put all the screenshots, files, images, notes, etc. all in one place under one task listing. I don't have to email her for updates because I can go look in Asana. No time wasting or interruptions necessary. I can invite clients or freelancers to use Asana for just those projects or tasks involving them. The search mechanism is extraordinary; if I need to go back and find something, it's really easy. **Slack** can also be an excellent tool for communication, creating channels, and inviting members to communicate in groups if it's not abused and doesn't become an instant chat and concentration disruptor. Whatever you decide to use is fine, *just don't use your inbox and don't abuse instant message.*

When I work with companies that use Outlook, I'm surprised how many of them have access to Microsoft Teams and don't use it. Often it's because they haven't been trained. It's a pet peeve of mine for companies to upgrade their tools and not provide training for their employees. Use the power of your systems—otherwise, you are wasting precious dollars and time.

> **I will implement a new or learn to use my existing task management system.**

DECLUTTER: Office

If you have an office or work from home, this one is essential. Yes, I've heard the Einstein quote, "If a cluttered desk is a sign of a cluttered mind, of what, then, is an empty desk a sign?" But I like my clean standing desk, thank you very much! Plus, it's not empty. I place only the most intentional items on my physical desktop. Figure out what you need to be accessible most of the time and what inspires your creative mind. Then show Einstein who's boss!

Novice: Physical Desktop

I like clean lines, minimal clutter, and things to be organized. I have a narrow standing desk with a small surface space, so

I can't have too much stuff around. This suits my personality. Other people may like a desk full of everything where they can see it all out on the surface. I'm not going to force you to get rid of all of your things. I am going to ask you to be intentional.

Start by taking every single thing off of your desk and putting everything in a box. Now, one by one, put what you need handy at all times back on the desk until it starts to feel that it's just enough. Enough that it feels like your workspace, but not so much it starts to feel cluttered. The things you only use occasionally (a stapler for me) can be put in a drawer. The desk is for what you need accessible regularly.

Get in the habit of clearing your desk of unnecessary items at the end of each workday (before or after you decide on your Top Three Priorities for the next day) as a transition away from work. That way, when you start the next day, you aren't distracted by things that aren't necessary.

> *I will clear my desk once and put back everything that I need accessible. At the end of each day or week (minimally), I will clear my desk of clutter. I am not attempting to be clutter-free. I am maximizing my workspace and being intentional about what is on it.*

Pro: *Supplies*

I used to hoard office supplies for years. I have the same box of staples I bought about a decade ago. My paper clips have moved to three different houses. Part of the problem is that I can't buy just what I need. A box of 25 staples or paper clips isn't an option. It's a box of 100 and they just take up valuable drawer real estate. One thing I encouraged when I managed a team of 18 was for them to share supplies. For example, when someone purchased one box of 100 paper clips, they would split it with their desk neighbor. A box of 50 envelopes would last me a year, so I shared them with another manager.

If you have supplies you rarely use, donate them to a school or non-profit. Check all your pens. Get rid of the ones that don't work or that don't feel nice to write with (pretty much every hotel pen I've ever picked up). Paperless office? Why do you still have that three-ring hole punch? A student or association may be able to use those supplies that have been in your desk collecting dust and taking up valuable drawer real estate for years.

> *I will go through all my office supplies and only keep what I will be able to use in one year.*

Master: *Inspiration*

I'm all for a functional workspace, but I also like inspiration. There are a few things on my desk that I find joy in or that are special to me. Some people don't care about this, but if you do, look at what is on your desk and discriminate until you only have what truly inspires you or is functional.

Here is what is on top of my desk currently:

- Primer book with my goals and visions for the year (use daily, functional, and inspirational)

- Notebook for handwritten notes (use daily, functional)
- One pen
- Laptop (use daily, functional)
- An external monitor (use daily, functional)
- Mr. Coffee Coffee Warmer (use daily, functional)
- Phone and AirPod charger (use daily, functional)
- An oyster shell (gift from my business coach, inspirational)
- Texas doorknob (gift from Texas Business Travel Association, inspirational and functional because it acts as a fidget gadget)
- Stone from Temazcal ceremony in Huatulco, Mexico (inspiration and fidget gadget)
- Apprentice organizer with various things inside

That's it!

> *I will consider what is truly inspirational to me and only have those things on my desk that spark creativity or motivate me to do my best work.*

HEALTH: Processed Foods

Take this opportunity to trade in your processed foods for whole foods. Your body and mind will thank you. This is one of the best healthy changes you can make for yourself. If you regularly eat processed foods with ingredients you can't pronounce, it's time to figure out substitutes that you enjoy. It may take some extra planning at first and experimenting to find what works for you, but you are worth more than a chemical-filled, microwaved frozen dinner!

Novice: Processed Food Swap-Out

Did you know that your chemically-concocted, boxed, frozen delicacy that says it's healthy is setting you up for sabotage? What the heck are whole foods anyway? Isn't it just a grocery store chain?

The terms "whole foods" and "clean eating" are buzzwords that are becoming diluted in the same way that Paleo somehow can mean energy bars. (Were cavemen and cavewomen really sitting around munching on these things?) The definitions are blurry and vary from person-to-person and company-to-company. Instead of worrying if you are eating "clean," think about buying and eating food in its natural state. If it comes in a box, semi-cooked, with sauces already over it, it's not a whole food. It's more likely a chemical concoction that has been subtly, or not so subtly, processed to make it easier to digest.

What's the problem with easier to digest?

We eat more of it.

Food scientists know that if food is already broken down, we'll consume more. These processed foods also often contain high levels of sodium, sugar, and additives that increase flavor.

- A study by Barr and Wright in 2010 comparing energy expenditure after eating processed foods versus eating whole foods found a decreased calorie burn rate of 47 percent.[1]

That's right, eating processed foods reduces the number of calories burned by 47 percent!

This means you will gain more weight eating 100 calories of French fries than you will eating 100 calories of baked potato. You'll gain more weight with 100 calories of white bread than 100 calories of millet or quinoa. Also, if you trade applesauce for apples, you'll definitely consume more because it has already been broken down and is more comfortable to slurp. The science couldn't be clearer. If you want to gain weight or put on pounds, it's simple. Eat more highly-processed foods.

Calories in are not calories out. A calorie is a measurable unit of energy, but depending on the source, it's not processed or used the same way in our bodies. I had an engineer argue with me that weight loss was simple. Calories in = calories out. He wasn't open to hearing about how foods are digested, how hormones are involved, and how gut flora impacts weight loss. Fiber requires more work and therefore is less easily-absorbed, for instance. More passes through our bodies without sticking around (on our hips and butt). Processed food doesn't feed our gut microbiomes the same way as unprocessed foods. The microbiome is hot research now because of the link between good gut bacteria and being at a healthy weight and the lack of some beneficial bacteria being linked to obesity, diabetes, autoimmune diseases, and mental illness. I even became certified as a *Gut Health Specialist* through the **Institute of Integrative Nutrition** because I was so fascinated by what I've learned. Want more? Check out the book *10% Human: How your body's microbes hold the key to health and happiness.*

How a food is cooked, if at all, can also determine how a food is digested. We may only absorb about two-thirds of the total calories in a raw starch as opposed to a cooked starch. Even a starch that has been cooked and cooled (like rice or potatoes that have been refrigerated for about twelve hours) has fewer digestible enzymes, i.e., resistant starch, so your body will not process as many calories as it would if it you ate those starches hot right out of the pot. Resistant starch isn't transformed and absorbed as quickly in the bloodstream. This is a bonus of food prepping and cooking foods like rice or quinoa early in the week and reheating them as leftovers. The American Chemical Society found that adding a teaspoon of coconut oil to the boiling water before adding the rice, and then refrigerating it for about twelve hours increased the ratio of resistant starch by at least ten times, resulting in 50 to 60 percent fewer calories absorbed! Don't worry, you don't have to eat it cold. It still works reheated. Side bonus: resistant starch helps feed your gut bacteria too![2]

When our guts don't have to work as hard, we'll eat more food. That's why you can down a bag of Cheetos and still want to get your orange-dusted fingers on something substantial.

Much like a child should know what a real chicken leg looks like and that chickens don't come with fingers or nuggets, we should know what vegetables look like before they've been cooked, mashed, or beaten to a pulp. I grew up in a house where the only things "plant-based" were the house plants and didn't know what most veggies looked like in their natural state. (I still can't tell the difference between a rutabaga and a turnip to save my life.)

It turns out, green beans and Brussel sprouts are actually crunchy, not mushy.

Potatoes and carrots come in different colors—orange, purple, white, and red.

And peppers taste and look different depending on when they are picked.

But who has time to wash, chop, and prep, right? Start small. Frozen veggies and fruits are often just as good as fresh. Sometimes they're even better because they are frozen at the peak of ripeness. As long as they aren't sugared or syruped to death or tossed in some kind of fake cheese-food sauce, they can work.

Buy fruits and veggies already chopped up on the salad bar or at the grocery store. Yes, it's more expensive, but so are medicines, buying new, bigger pants, and doctor bills. Also, if you buy produce already chopped up, make sure to cook and eat them within a day or two because once they've been chopped up, they will spoil more quickly than if they were whole.

Try one switch from processed food in the next month. Those six crackers that come in a sealed packet that you grabbed from a box that came in another box and still probably another bigger box could be switched out for something that you could have picked, pulled, or peeled off of a tree, vine, or root.

Here are some other ideas for easy substitutes to get you started:

- Steel cut oats instead of instant oatmeal
- Sliced cucumbers or peppers to dip instead of chips
- Baked sweet potato wedges instead of French fries
- Sparkling water with a splash of fruit juice instead of soda
- Homemade salad dressing (tahini and lemon juice or high-quality vinegar and oil) instead of bottled full-of-sugar-and-rancid-oil dressings)

- A hamburger you cooked instead of a boxed slider with high fructose corn syrup, soy flour, caramel color, and a list of other ingredients you can't pronounce
- Real guacamole made from avocados instead of processed "guacamole dip" (Dean's brand has only 2 percent real avocado and is filled with thickeners and dyes!)

> *I will substitute these foods* _____, _____, and _____ *for unprocessed or whole-food versions.*

Pro: *Whole Food Day*

Now that you've started substituting less-processed or whole foods into your diet, it's time to practice a Whole Foods Day. People respond differently to specific diets due to a myriad of reasons like genes, activity levels, gender, age, and disease indications. I'm the leanest I've ever been on a 45 to 50 percent carbohydrates, 35 to 40 percent fat, 20 to 25 percent protein diet, but this works for me due to my genetics (I've taken a couple of different gene profiles) and my autoimmune diseases. Genetically, a higher intake of fat doesn't contribute to weight gain for me as long as the number of overall calories align with my activity and energy levels. I also attribute my leanness to the fact that I don't get hungry as often and don't feel the need to snack all the time with my whole foods diet since it's so high in fiber from vegetables, fruits, and legumes and because it includes healthy fats. When I ate a much more processed, simple carbohydrate diet, I ate constantly. Now we know that snacking all day isn't as good for us as we thought, and there was never any reliable research to prove it was good for us to begin with.

No matter what the diet is—Paleo, Whole30, low-fat, vegetarian, Atkins, Zone, Ketogenic, or South Beach—none of them will tell you to eat more processed foods, unless of course the "article" you are reading is sponsored by a company that makes frozen or processed meals!

Try eating as many whole foods as you can for one day each week this month. Eat as few things pre-made or out of a box that you are heating up or thawing out as possible. This doesn't mean that frozen veggies or fruit is cheating or a pre-made salad you picked up from the grocery store (nix the pre-made dressing) won't count. Instead of automatically eliminating anything frozen, think about eating foods with as few ingredients as possible. Peanut butter should have peanuts and maybe salt. It doesn't need to have peanuts, sugar, and partially hydrogenated oil. Have grilled chicken instead of thinly sliced deli chicken, which is filled with chemical preservatives and sodium. See the example from the Novice habit section regarding guacamole with real avocados.

> *I will eat as many whole foods as close to their natural state as possible one day per week.*

Master: Whole Food Week

For the advanced challenge, try eating whole foods for one entire week this month. Most people can go for a day, but eating primarily whole foods for an entire week can show you just how many processed foods you consume. To set yourself up for success, think about your menu plan. Have everything you need on hand and prep what you can ahead of time. Make a stew or casserole from scratch, grill your proteins, chop your veggies, and roast, steam, or bake to reheat throughout the week. Also, consider what restaurants you might go out to. Take a look at their menu online and decide ahead of time what you can eat or else avoid eating out altogether during your whole food week.

Yes, this may take some time out of your schedule, but eating like this is so much better for your health, allows you to appreciate your food, and will challenge you to think more about what you put into your mouth. Intentional rather than mindless eating is the goal.

If you need a specific meal plan, I would advise something like **Whole30** which gives you recipes to try. Note that Whole30 isn't considered a long-term diet. That's why it's called Whole30 (i.e., 30 days). It's a great reset and education diet to help you think outside of your meal-planning box. If you have been diagnosed with an autoimmune disease and want to experiment with the Autoimmune Paleo diet, I recommend working with a coach like Dr. Ludy de Menten for support to get through the program. **https://www.healthy-withludy.com/**

> *I will choose one week this month to eat as many whole foods as possible.*

REFERENCES IN THIS CHAPTER

[1] https://www.ncbi.nlm.nih.gov/pubmed/20613890

[2] https://www.acs.org/content/acs/en/pressroom/newsreleases/2015/march/new-low-calorie-rice-could-help-cut-rising-obesity-rates.html

MONTH EIGHT

PRODUCTIVITY: Meetings

I know. "Marcey, what do you mean meetings aren't productive? How else am I supposed to create team cohesion in my office?" Sure, it's important for colleagues to meet face-to-face or via video chat from time to time. But when we fall into a default pattern of having meetings for the sake of having meetings, they lose their value. Take this opportunity to evaluate the value of the meetings you have. By all means if a meeting is truly productive, keep it!

Novice: Cancel the Default

Many of my clients in corporate happen to work for companies where they have meetings back to back, without any break, for six hours at a time. They get tasks they are supposed to complete during their meetings yet no white space in their calendars to complete them. They are often hired for their strategy or subject matter expertise, but they get no time to develop either.

Dear Corporate, would you please stop scheduling useless meetings?

When I give my Productivity Scorecards to groups to tailor their workshops, I ask how often they multitask during a meeting. The majority do so in over 50 percent of their meetings, and the ones who say they don't are often being dishonest. If you can multitask and check your email during a meeting then you do NOT need to be at that meeting.

First and foremost, stop defaulting to accepting meetings. Is it vital for you to attend? Could you read the minutes? Can you only attend part of it? I'm sure everyone has been in a teleconference that lasted an hour, only five minutes of which were relevant.

Try to end meetings at 1:45, 2:45, etc. instead of defaulting to the hour block. This gives people a chance to actually stand up, use the bathroom, and get a drink of water. It also keeps you from waiting for a few minutes for people to join the call or get to your meeting. If you just need to touch base with someone, schedule 10 or 15 minutes.

In my current business, I try to meet with people first by phone and then determine if it is worth my time to meet face-to-face. Owning your own business results in a lot of "meeting over coffee." I found that coffee shop meetings were a waste of money and time as they only led to something that couldn't be done over the phone maybe 15 percent of the time. I know I have offended some people by saying I don't meet face-to-face under most circumstances, but when people insist on meeting face-to-face all the time, I question how successful they are to have that much open time in their calendar! Not every networking opportunity is fruitful.

To be the master of your calendar, take a look at it a month out and look first at your recurring meetings. Determine which ones are genuinely required. If you are the person running them, see if they can be done less frequently or if they can be done in a shorter time frame. People tend to keep going with the same frequency and time of meetings, even when they don't need to. Can a meeting be done once a week for 15 minutes instead of 30? Can it be changed to every two weeks instead of weekly as the project is progressing?

> *I will not accept meetings mindlessly and will inquire about my purpose at the meeting. I will change any meetings that I am in charge of to less than one hour, i.e., 15, 25, or 45 minutes. I will reconsider any meeting I join where I am multitasking and ask to be removed from the attendee list.*

Pro: Standing Meetings

If you want to be memorable, perform standing meetings. When people have to stand in a room for a meeting, they naturally get through the agenda much faster because most people don't want to stand around for an hour. Making participants slightly uncomfortable physically combined with an environment not being amenable to electronics makes for a much more productive meeting.

- A study from Washington University found that standing meetings boosted excitement around the creative process and reduced people's defensiveness.[1]

One of my former clients, Emaar Properties, has meeting rooms with a high-top table and no chairs, requiring participants to stand. I've also seen several start-up incubators with meeting rooms with no tables and chairs. A design firm in Toronto makes all meetings fewer than 30 minutes and their morning huddles as standing meetings.

> *I will schedule standing meetings if they are less than _____ minutes.*

Master: *Scheduling System*

There are many scheduling systems on the market that allow people to see available blocks on your calendar and request an appointment. If you spend your time doing the email dance to schedule a simple appointment, start using a system. Having a simple link saves about 12 minutes of scheduling back-and-forth for each meeting scheduled. After five meetings, you've saved yourself about an hour.

Check out systems like **Acuity** (my preferred), **Schedule Once**, or **Calendly**. You can create different lengths and locations of meetings and sync meetings with your Google and Outlook calendars so you never have to post your availability. In my set-up, you can choose from four different meetings with me—Speaker Inquiry, Discovery Session, Virtual Coffee, or 45-minute coaching session. I include my link in every email in my signature line as well as on my website. Here is an example of an email with my scheduling link in the content.

Hi Jim,

It was great to meet you on Thursday. I would appreciate a quick chat on the phone to talk about the project you requested. Please use my scheduling link (HYPERLINK TO SCHEDULER) to find a time that is convenient for us both.

Assistant.to is another great tool and happens to be free for Gmail users. It allows you to embed your availability directly into the email. You can choose from different lengths of meetings, locations, and whether phone, web conference, or face-to-face is preferred. The email recipient can select a time that works for them without ever closing the email. The downside is it only lets you pick times for three different days. I use Assistant.to for one-off meetings or meetings taking place within the next couple of weeks. If a person takes too long to get back to your email, the times you allocated to them may already be gone. Right now, it only works with Gmail and G Suite calendars.

For families, I recommend a shared Google Calendar. You can turn off your other family members when you only want to see your appointments and turn on their calendars when you want to see them all at once. I use this with my husband, who has a calendar for teaching and music gigs. I can check the calendar and make plans without consulting him. He can also look at my calendar and see when I'm out of town or in meetings. We invite each other to events and even on dates this way.

> *I will implement a scheduling system to eliminate the back-and-forth to schedule a meeting.*

DECLUTTER: Kitchen

The kitchen is another room in the house we might not immediately think to declutter. This is especially true if you have a big kitchen with enough cabinets and drawers to house all of your utensils, spices, and kitchen gadgets. If you have a smaller kitchen, you may have no choice but to pare down. Consider how much time and effort it would save you to optimize your kitchen for organization. If you read the processed foods section in the previous chapter and realized you don't eat many whole foods because it takes so long to chop and prep, then maybe decluttering your kitchen will help. I like to cook, but if cooking isn't fast and easy, I'm not going to do it. Decluttering my kitchen has made a huge difference for me.

Novice: Utensil Drawer

Kitchens tend to house unitaskers: items we purchased when we felt ambitious about making everything from scratch, decorative platters and bowls we don't use, and the proverbial junk that lands in junk drawers. I always thought I needed a bigger kitchen, but what I really needed was to get rid of the things I wasn't using. I started with my utensil drawer.

I decided to take everything out of my utensil drawer for 30 days and put it all inside a box on my table. If I used an item, I put it back in the drawer. Whatever was left in the box after that month was donated. I had utensils I couldn't even name and didn't know what they were used for. I got honest with myself. If a recipe calls for zesting a lemon and I'm most likely not going to do it, it's not worth keeping a unitasking zester around. Instead of freshly squeezing a lime, I'll buy a bottle of lime juice at the grocery store. How many stainless steel straws could one person possibly need? How many times have you used that fondue set you got for your wedding ten years ago? A friend of mine got rid of her giant plastic 24-cupcake container and borrows one from a neighbor to make her kids birthday cupcakes twice a year.

I do cook a lot from scratch, but I'm simple and don't want to open a drawer and have to sort through it. If you use a zester regularly, by all means, knock yourself out. I still bet there are things you could toss or give to someone who can use them.

> *I will go through all my utensils and get rid of any that are broken, cracked, I don't know what it is used for, or I haven't used it in a year.*

Pro: Condiments and Spices

When I go to someone's house and see a cabinet full of spices, some with dust on them, or an entire refrigerator door's worth of condiments, I tend to just skip them altogether. Most people cannot go through that many seasonings and spices in a timely enough manner that they are still edible or tasty.

Spices can last a long time, but they eventually lose their potency. As a general rule, whole spices will last for about four years, ground for two or three years, and dried herbs for one to three years. Spices won't go rancid, but they may be taking up real estate in your cabinet. How many of you have the Lazy Susan or rotating spice rack full of herbs you can't pronounce, let alone remember what recipe you bought them for originally? Instead, only keep the spices that you will actually use and enjoy. If you only need a little of something for a new recipe, bottle or bag up half of it and give it to a friend to try. I also like buying from a bulk bin so I only get what I need.

Condiments definitely go bad. I like the websites **www.stilltasty.com** or eatbydate.com. Do a once-over of your fridge and get rid of old sauces that smell funny or are past their shelf life. If you buy something you won't eat a lot of, split that with a friend too! I love Trader Joe's wasabi mayonnaise, but it would take me way too long to eat an entire jar, so I split it with my mom. I do the same with jams and jellies because I don't eat sweet condiments often. I bottle half into something smaller and give it to a friend.

You can also clean sweep all those unhealthy, sugary, highly-processed condiments that are sabotaging your nutrition, i.e., bottled salad dressings, high-sodium soy sauce, and ketchup and barbecue sauce with high-fructose corn syrup.

> *I will do a clean sweep of my old spices and unhealthy or expired condiments and vow to share if I buy too much of something and can't use it all within a reasonable time.*

Master: *Professional Organizer*

A Professional Organizer can be an angel descending upon your house and seeing all the dysfunctional ways you use your space. I am a firm believer in inviting someone in to help you get control of your clutter or create a more functional environment. I am an organized person, but I wanted to experience working with a professional organizer to see if I could better use my space and to find someone to refer my clients to. I hired Nancy Haworth of On Task Organizing (who also works virtually) and in four hours, we covered my entire house (unusual, but I was already starting from a good place). She found several things that my husband and I could change to make us more efficient, and when we were done, I had removed four boxes of stuff we realized we didn't need from our kitchen.

> *Everyday items I see people keep that they don't need or use are wedding gifts of kitchen items. They take up valuable space in a kitchen for decades. If you haven't used these gifts after a couple of years, assess if you will ever use them and if that space could be better served to hold things you use and need in the kitchen.*
> — *Nancy Haworth, On Task Organizing*

You may have a friend or family member who loves to organize or you might want to invest in a certified professional organizer from the **National Association of Productivity and Organizing Professionals**. A certified Professional Organizer has completed an exam and over 1,500 hours of paid organization work. It is no joke. There's a lot more to organizing than getting your giggles at the Container Store.

While you may not be able to afford one for your entire house, investing in the most overwhelming or cluttered area can be useful. You can also start with the Netflix series, **Tidying Up With Marie Kondo,** based on the bestselling book *The Life-Changing Magic of Tidying Up* or check out the books

Unclutter Your Life in One Week and *Outer Order, Inner Calm.*

> I will invest in a professional, watch a series, or read a book on decluttering and start with one area or room in my house.

HEALTH: Convenient and Healthy Foods

Now that your kitchen has been decluttered, you're ready to tackle healthy foods. You've done the whole foods day and the whole foods week, but now you're ready to make healthy eating even more of a habit. This section's tips will help you realize this dream. We'll start with food prep and planning. Yes, this is key to keeping you from reaching for processed foods. If you can make healthy food as convenient as those processed foods, you'll be much more likely to reach for the healthy stuff when you are tired and just want to eat something quick and easy. That's where we're headed. Let's go!

Novice: Prep and Plan

Food planning and prepping, even if you aren't the one doing it, is essential to sticking to a healthy meal plan. One of the biggest reasons people report not eating a healthy diet is time. Convenience is critical, but that doesn't have to mean you eat processed foods or don't get in enough servings of vegetables daily.

First, planning out even a few meals a week can help with decision-fatigue and reduce making poor choices when you get home at night, super-hungry, and reach for whatever can be reheated in 30 seconds. Prepping food one day a week—for most people, a weekend day—can feed you multiple times throughout the week if you eat leftovers. If you don't want to make entire meals, at least wash and chop all of your veggies and fruits so you can throw them into whatever you've prepared. Purchase a blackboard or use blackboard paint or a whiteboard or whiteboard decal and put it in your kitchen so the family sees the plan for the week. Create themes like Meat-Free Monday, Tuesday Taco Night, or Sunday Brunch to make it easier to plan.

Don't like to chop? Buy fruit and veggies frozen (always ready to eat) or pre-chopped at the grocery store. I've heard people complain that pre-chopped vegetables and fruit are too expensive at the grocery store, yet they'll go out for dinner instead and spend four times as much. How does that make economic sense?

Here are some of the things I might do for a Sunday meal prep:

- Bake, roast, steam, or sauté vegetables to throw in whatever I fix throughout the week (e.g., salad, rice, eggs)
- Make a crockpot stew, chili, or soup
- Grill, roast, or bake proteins like chicken, beef, and fish and boil eggs
- Make five or six muesli bowls for my husband and two days of smoothie bowls for me
- Brew Teeccinno to mix with iced coffee

Prepping drastically cuts down on poor choices at the end of the day when I'm tired or at lunch when I don't have a lot of time. I spend about one hour (yes, only an hour because I don't do the chopping myself, which I'll discuss in the Outsourcing section) on Sunday to set myself up for success the rest of the week.

I'm also a big fan of making big batches of food and freezing them in weekly portions. This also cuts back on clean-up. At least half the time I make a dish, I double it so I can have leftovers or send it with my husband the next day. Here are some food ideas to cook once and eat twice (or three or four times!):

- Stews, chilis, and soups – After cooling, freeze in gallon or quart-size freezer bags or reusable silicone bags.

- Casseroles – I make a casserole I call Burrito Bake and divide it into two or three containers to freeze. Then I can thaw one for a fast meal. This has also become my go-to when I need to provide meals for friends who have recently moved or are going through a hard time where they would appreciate having a meal they don't have to cook.

- Any kind of muffin or bread-like product that you can take out of the freezer the night before to eat the next day – Making a few dozen power muffins to wrap and remove individually is perfect and much better than grabbing a processed granola bar on your way out the door.

- Cookies, cupcakes, and brownies – These can be batched and frozen, so you only eat one or two at a time instead of all of them.

If you need help learning how to properly prep or batch food, try **Cooksmarts**. It not only gives you recipe ideas but also provides you with a grocery list (minus what you've checked off that you already have at home), shows you how to prep the food for the week, and gives ideas for leftovers.

> *I will make these recipes* _____ *on a weekly basis to freeze and thaw to eat later.*

Pro: *Meal Subscription Services*

Meal subscription services like **Hello Fresh** and **Blue Apron** have become all the rage in the last few years, and I've tried a few myself. I'll start with the downside: the waste. Packaging up all of that food into a box with cooler packs leaves us with more waste in the landfill. However, the cooler packs can be reused or donated to non-profit food relief programs, schools for field trips, elderly services since they sometimes have to transport medications on ice, and community supported agriculture services. Buying from these larger subscription services also doesn't support the local farmers in your area.

What about the upside? There are many. Meal subscriptions are perfect for people who are learning to cook and don't know how to prepare food. Everything you would need, down to a single garlic clove, is included along with instructions for exactly how to make the dish. Each week the service delivers three different complete meals in a box for two or four people, but you will most likely have leftovers (my husband and I often do). One of my clients invests in one meal kit a month and has her teens assist in the kitchen so they can learn how to make dinner.

My CSA program, Papa Spuds, includes a few recipe kits every week where I have to add a few of my own ingredients to the veggies they deliver to make complete meals. I love these because they are typically dishes I wouldn't make on my own, and the recipes are fun to try using local ingredients.

I've used subscription services in the following ways:

- As a treat once a month to try something new

- When traveling to a cabin or house where I'm vacationing or on business – I can have the boxes delivered directly and cook them myself instead of worrying about hitting a grocery store when I get to my destination.

- As a "house warming" gift for people who have recently moved – This helps them have food to prepare at home.

Other types of services include ready-made meals that you can order and buy in individual servings weekly from restaurant chains like **Clean Eatz, Muscle Maker Grill,** or my local favorite, **Living Fit.** This is perfect for those who want to track their nutritional needs carefully and buy several pre-packaged (but fresh) meals all at once. When I was in a bike accident, one of my dear friends gave me the fabulous gift of a week's worth of meals because she knew with my arm in a sling, it would be harder for me to cook, and she knew how important my nutrition would be while I was healing.

> *I will try one subscription service to expand my imagination or for the convenience of having everything delivered.*

Master: *Personal Chef*

Before you skip over this section because you think it may be too fancy for you, stick with me. I am not a fancy-pants nor would I consider myself elite. We all spend money differently. One thing that I consider an investment is having a house assistant come in once per week. I'll talk more about this in Month Eleven, but for now, I'll share the following. For my weekly investment, my assistant chops and preps all the produce that is delivered in my CSA. This has significantly increased both how often I eat at home and the joy I get from making my own meals. I really do like to cook and I prefer to eat at home, but I don't like to chop. While some people may balk at paying someone to do meal prep (she spends maybe an hour on food), if my husband and I were to go out once or twice a week, we would spend more than what we pay our house assistant. I would rather invest in her than go out to eat since I really do like eating at home.

- House Assistant – two hours of food prep for $50 that gives us meals or meal prep for an entire week.

- A meal at B.Good (fast, casual restaurant) where two entrees, two sides, and two drinks will cost about $34.50 plus there is the 30-minute round trip and 10-minute wait.

I have friends and clients who have someone come to their

houses weekly or monthly and make several dishes in one session. Others have someone who will grocery shop for them. I use **Instacart** and Amazon Subscribe and Save to have all of my groceries delivered, so I don't need this. Instacart charges 10 percent of the bill, but I would have spent more than that buying stuff on a whim in the store, and then there's the time spent going to the store and shopping. The Instacart fee feels more than worth it.

Another option might be joining a cooking circle. I have a friend who has a circle with five other houses in their neighborhood. They each take turns making large batches of food and having them ready for pick-up at their homes. This is a way to get home-cooked meals without doing it all yourself.

Some personal chefs will do meal planning, shopping, cooking, and clean-up. Don't confuse a personal chef with a private chef, who is an employee. Personal chefs may require a minimum number of meals be prepared at a time or may prepare them at their own facility and have them ready for pick-up or drop off. You could use a website like **care.com** (more on this below in the Personal Outsourcing section) to create a specific job description and find exactly what works for you and your family. You also can pool your resources with friends or neighbors and hire someone who likes to cook to batch prepare meals for a group.

If this feels unreachable financially, consider what you would pay at a restaurant, including the time it takes to drive to your go-to spot and be waited on. How much would a personal chef save you in the cost of going out or wasted food that you buy but don't have time to prepare and eat?

Additionally, don't be afraid to get creative here. Maybe you could barter with a friend who likes to cook. Do you love styling clothes and could put together outfits in exchange for five meals? Could you be a handyperson for a couple of hours while they make a few batches of their famous protein pancakes and Mediterranean casserole?

> *I will test out a personal chef, cooking circle, or barter for home-cooked meals one time this month.*

REFERENCES IN THIS CHAPTER

[1] https://journals.sagepub.com/doi/abs/10.1177/1948550614538463

MONTH NINE

PRODUCTIVITY: Switchtasking

Productive multitasking is a myth much like the earth is flat, squats are "bad" for your knees, baldness comes from the mother's side, and humans only use 10 percent of their brains. But it's important to define "multitasking" further before we can understand why it's not productive. There are different kinds of tasking. For example, there is background tasking with the primary task where each task is using a different part of the brain to do multiple things like listening to a podcast while running or an audiobook while cooking. Background tasking is not the same as multitasking because doing two things like cooking and listening to an audio book don't compete for brain space. I can stir a pot or put one foot in front of the other and still hear and comprehend words or music. What I can't do is listen to a conversation and read words at the same time. I can't watch a movie and work on my laptop. Something is getting lost because the words coming in through our ears and eyes or out of our mouth must go through the *same* cognitive channel in the prefrontal cortex to be comprehended.[1] This is why multitasking is unproductive.

When we try to watch TV and work at the same time, for example, one of these tasks gets the short end of the stick causing the dumber part of our brain to respond, and we can't choose which task gets that part of the brain. Constant switchtasking (going between two tasks, which is really what we do when we "multitask") also creates decision-fatigue and lowers productivity by as much as 40 percent. It even reduces your IQ.[2]

And yeah—most people's brains can't listen to music with words and read an email at the same time.

Novice: Phone Calls

The first place to practice presence and focus in your life is during phone calls and virtual meetings. You know you do it. As soon as someone starts talking about something that doesn't directly involve your input, you switch tabs on your laptop or look at your phone to check email or social media. If it's evident to you when someone else is doing it, why do you think you are so masterful that others don't notice *you* not paying attention? It can be even harder to stay present during phone meetings than being in-person because the person on the other end of the line can't see what you're doing. To change this habit, start by choosing a call or virtual meeting where you usually drift over to reading your email at the same time and stay present instead. Sign out of email, move or turn your chair away from your desk, or do what I do and go for a walk or pace the room. Our eyes can't help but read what is in front of us. Shut it off and listen or you don't need to be on the call (see the productivity habit for month eight).

Practice your focus on calls. If you are in multiple calls or virtual meetings a day, start with being intentional about your focus during at least one meeting. And if you are someone who is distracted even during face-to-face meetings, start there first!

> *I will listen on* _____ *call or virtual meeting and not do anything that involves reading at the same time.*

Pro: Singletask on a Project or Task

Switchtasking between multiple screens and thought processes slows us down. When we try to work on multiple tasks or projects simultaneously, each with a different end goal, our attention gets pulled in different directions. This can cause our brains to go into overdrive. Take a look at the following examples to see the difference between effective and ineffective methods.

An example of switchtasking that can work:

I have three screens open: Gmail, PowerPoint, and Asana. I read an email about the Macon proposal and what they need. I add the details for the Macon team in PowerPoint. I enter tasks in Asana, my task management system, for my assistant to complete a resource guide about the Macon presentation. Why this works: I'm only thinking about Macon and the ultimate goal is to get their presentation done. Each of the three tasks gets me closer to that goal.

Ineffective switchtasking:

I read the Macon email, send an invoice to Baker and Company, read an email from a coaching client, send a Voxer, work on a presentation for Butterfield Brewery, and then go back to the Macon email again. Why this doesn't work: none of these things has anything to do with the others, and each time I switch, my brain has to change gears, remember what I did on the project before, then figure out what needs to be done next. This will always result in losing time. I'm never getting into a flow state where I'm fully concentrating and focused on the task in front of me.

This month I want you to work on *singletasking*, solely focusing on completing one task or completing one focused sprint time each day. For a concentrated sprint time, the minimum would be 25 minutes (a Pomodoro), which might be tough for some attention spans and the maximum would be 90 minutes before taking a break and stepping away from the computer to prevent glute amnesia. You also could opt to sign up for a **Focus90 session** with me at **www.marceyrader. com/Focus90**. As a reminder, each session is a 90-minute work sprint over Zoom virtual conferencing where we sign in with cameras on and sound off. I give a productivity tip and then we state our intention of what we will get done in the chat box. For 80 minutes we bust out our tasks and then when the time is up, I restate the productivity tip, and we each report in chat what we were able to achieve. It's free!

> *I will singletask each day for ___ minutes or on these tasks _____.*

Master: Nuclear Options

Sometimes we just need to save ourselves from ourselves (revisit the Squirrel Blockers habit from Month Six) and use nuclear options. The world would be a more productive place if we all could admit that self-discipline is generally low and that we don't have the willpower not to check Facebook, see what that flashing notification is, or check the weather one more time. We are not smarter than the people who create these channels. They hire people whose life's work is to study what it takes to get that dopamine drip going and capture our attention. That's why we need to keep some nuclear options in mind.

Freedom.to is a program that allows you to block specific websites or types of websites (social media, news channels, shopping, etc.) for set periods or regularly. It works across all devices. If you try to go to one of those websites on any device during your Freedom block, you'll only see a green screen with a butterfly reminding you that you are free from distraction. I love this program and use it Monday through Saturday from eight p.m. to nine a.m. on my email (because email is never my Top Task) and all day on Sunday to remind me to take a day off and not check email out of boredom. I also block social media and Amazon, and when I'm in a writing session, I will prevent myself from entering all programs on my computer except for Grammarly and Google Docs.

Rescue Time allows you to block distracting websites, set productivity goals for the day, and even track offline activity.

Inbox Pause and **Inbox When Ready**, which we covered in Month Three, can help reduce inbox distractions.

Facebook Feed Eradicator is a Chrome extension that will replace your news feed with an inspirational quote. You then have to intentionally type in a name or a business to see their posts.

Stay Focused and **Moment.to** are app blockers which help you focus by restricting the usage of blocked apps or your whole phone. You can choose your own usage limit based on a daily usage limit, hourly usage limit, a limit on the number of launches, specified time intervals, or a limit on the number of phone screen unlocks.

Why waste your willpower on something that you can arrange to block for as long as you want?

> *I will install and test one blocker to remove distractions and allow me to focus.*

DECLUTTER: Media and Electronics

The physical media and electronics we have stashed around our homes can make the rooms where we try to relax feel cluttered and heavy. With timed obsolescence being so prevalent in our digital world, it can feel like as soon as you buy a new device, it's outdated. Then what do you do with that dinosaur? Sure, some people still have an eight-track player in the basement that they like to show off to their grandkids, but unless you're hoping to turn your basement into a museum, you can probably let go of all those old media players and electronics. And those paper manuals? I have two words: recycle bin.

Novice: Manuals

For those readers under the age of thirty, you may need to Google what a manual is, but for the rest of us, we were given paper books or instructions with every device we purchased. It was a colossal waste of paper because they typically included instructions in multiple languages, text was written in small print, and they were not always easy or all that helpful to read anyway. Some people prefer to go through a manual step-by-step before even plugging in the device, and others will play with it until they figure it out. Many items do not come with manuals now, and even when they do, how many people actually look at them? You can always search online and in most cases, a helpful person has even made a video describing how to use the device, answering any question you might have. By the way, the same also goes for the instructions for board games.

We don't need manuals taking up precious real estate anymore in our drawers, cupboards, and binders. Unless you have something so old it can't be found online, chuck it. Think about how you typically search or learn something and if you are someone who rarely or never picks up a manual, get rid of it and open that space up for something else. And for the love of unicorns, please throw out your manuals for items you no longer have!

I will recycle all manuals I don't need and will probably search online anyway when I do need instructions or help.

Pro: Electronic Media

Electronic media includes television, radio, Internet, fax, CD-ROM's, DVD's, and any other medium that requires electricity or digital encoding of information. We're going to address CD's, DVD's, cassettes, and VCR tapes first.

How many of you reading this still have cassettes and VCR tapes that you haven't played in two decades and probably will never play again? And what about those Blue-Ray discs, DVDs, and CDs? My husband and I haven't had anything that plays CDs in at least five years, and even the players in our cars have a phone holder in them, so the slot acts as a receptacle for the holder rather than a music player. What is making you hold onto those tapes and discs? You can't even sell them to used music or video stores anymore. If you don't have a player (and maybe even if you do, but haven't used it in ages), donate them.

Okay, but wait, I have the limited edition box set of *Lord of the Rings* and that's gotta be worth something, right? Um no. Limited edition means nothing when the technology is outdated. Trust me, we tried this ourselves and were shocked at the few bucks we could get for something that we paid extra for back in the day. If it's not going to be used again, get rid of it and open up that real estate.

> **I will donate, attempt to sell, or recycle my electronic media I can no longer play or won't play in the future.**

Master: *Electronic Players*

How many old iPods, CD players, DVD players, slow laptops, and headphones with knotted and frayed cords do you have laying around? Do you really need seven USB-A and five micro-USB cables? Take inventory of what you actually use and sell or donate what you don't use now before they are entirely worthless or no one will even take them.

iPod Shuffles can be donated to Music & Memory **https:// musicandmemory.org/** where they are given to adults with Alzheimer's Disease or dementia. I dare you to watch the documentary **Alive Inside** and still want to keep that old music player stashed in your drawer. If you still play CDs and DVDs, keep one player and get rid of any extra. A slow laptop is just that—a slow laptop. You won't get money for it, but you can donate it to different non-profits, like **Soldiers' Angels** that updates, refurbishes, and sends used laptops to VA hospitals. Check locally to see if you have a non-profit nearby that will accept your electronics.

Having one back-up tablet or laptop can be a good idea if you rely on your computer for work. Or you can do what I've done and spend $200 to purchase a Chromebook back-up if your computer goes down or if you feel better taking something less expensive when you travel or head to the coffee shop.

And all those cords? How many do you really need? I have extras, but at one point, I counted eight of the same type of cable. Unnecessary. Donate them to a hotel the next time you travel because who hasn't left their cord or cable at home?

> *Donate, sell, recycle, or toss unused or outdated electronics and accessories.*

HEALTH: Mindfulness

Mindfulness, a very popular buzzword right now, has been used to mean different things to different people.

Dictionary definitions:

* *The quality or state of being conscious or aware of something.*
* *A mental state achieved by focusing one's awareness on the present moment, while calmly acknowledging and accepting one's feelings, thoughts, and bodily sensations; used as a therapeutic technique.*

I started practicing mindfulness about six years ago and have worked my way through different techniques. Anyone who knows me personally would not describe me as woo-woo. Much like practicing yoga, experiencing the benefits of meditation for me depends on the teacher, style, and environment. Several major companies, including *The Huffington Post*, Goldman Sachs Group Inc., and Google have incorporated meditation training into their offerings for employees to help them focus, increase creativity, and expand emotional intelligence.

Meditation or deep-breathing is going to the gym for your soul. There are more than 18,000 published studies on the physical and mental benefits of meditation. (See, it's not woo-woo. It's science).

NIH studies[3] have shown a 23 percent decrease in mortality, a 30 percent decrease in death due to cardiovascular disease, and a reduction in cancer mortality in people who practice meditation. Is there a drug that does that?

Benefits of meditation and deep breathing techniques include:

- A lowered acute stress response
- An increased concentration of gray matter in the hippocampus of the brain, which is subject to the stress release of cortisol – The brain function of meditators is very different from that of non-meditators. Meditators have an enhanced capacity to concentrate and manage emotions.
- Reduced concentration of C-reactive protein that is associated with heart disease
- A decrease in active inflammation and an increase in the immune system
- Lower blood pressure
- Increased impulse control
- Improved attention
- Better sleep

Novice: 4-6-8 Breath

An easy way to start focusing on your breath is to practice a technique I call the "4-6-8 breath." I inhale for four counts, hold for six counts, and exhale for eight counts. I can do this anywhere and don't need my phone or an app. Focus on breathing into your belly, filling it with air and when exhaling, letting the air out of your belly up through your chest and out your mouth or nose. Keep your chest and shoulders level without letting them rise up and down. I do this 4-6-8 breathing technique every time I get in a vehicle, using the seat belt as my trigger. (Okay, I do forget occasionally, but the intention is every time to form a habit.) I typically do this for four to six cycles. It relaxes me if I'm rushed and helps me calm down before I start driving. I've also developed the habit of doing four cycles any time I'm waiting in public, i.e., in line, in an elevator, or waiting for an appointment before reaching for my phone out of boredom.

> *"The 4-6-8 breath works! It kept me calm during a bout with my crying baby!"* — *Andrea Pereira, Senior Human Resources Business Partner*

I will use _____ **as my trigger to practice 4 to 6 cycles of the 4-6-8 breath.**

Pro: *Gratitude Journal*

Gratitude research is an evolving field with fascinating results. The Harvard Mental Health Letter cites research showing that gratitude journaling has been found to increase positive emotions, improve sleep, increase feelings of compassion and kindness, and even strengthen the immune system.

I started gratitude journaling in 2013 and use the **5-minute journal app**. I list three things for which I'm grateful each morning and three ways I'm going to make that day great. Then, at the end of the day, I list three things about the day that were amazing, and one thing I could have done better.

The 5-minute journal app is one of my top five most recommended apps. You can even attach photos and make it into a photo journal. It's fun to look back on vacations and see my gratefuls, amazings, and pictures.

Journaling is best done when written down or entered in an app instead of just thought about in your head. It's also crucial that you don't let your gratitude get stale by stating the same thing every day. After a few days, your gratefulness for your cat kind of loses its meaning. Try to make it something new each day. Your gratitude statements don't have to be profound or broad, like "my health" or "my family." They can be straightforward like "They gave me extra guacamole at lunch today," "My spouse made the bed," or "My plane was on time."

Find a time of day where you can be consistent to do your journaling. I do mine first thing in the morning before I meditate and at night around seven or before my evening meditation. Thinking about what you are grateful for before you sleep can help ease any feelings of anxiety or overwhelm leftover from the day. If we let negative thoughts fester, they can seep into our subconscious mind while we sleep and get replayed throughout the night.

Greater Good in Action has excellent tips to start your gratitude journaling at **https://ggia.berkeley.edu/practice/ gratitude_journal**. One good tip is to get very specific detailing exactly why you are grateful for your spouse or that your dentist appointment resulted in no cavities!

A good friend of mine has a Gratitude Jar in her living room with paper and colored pens beside it. She invites anyone who is visiting her to write something they are grateful for, anonymous or not. Occasionally, she takes the papers out of the jar and reads them. I LOVE this and routinely write something for her jar when I visit. You could do this for yourself or with your family as a New Year's ritual: once a week or whenever you think of it throughout the year write something you're grateful for and place it in the jar, then just before you ring in the New Year, pull out each slip of paper and read the notes.

> **I will practice writing down three things I am grateful for every day.**

Master: *Meditation and Self-Hypnosis*

After several years of trying to meditate and beating myself up over not being successful, I installed an app on my smartphone from **Calm.com** and have managed to make using it a daily habit, with a streak of over 734 days at the time of this writing. I realized what I needed was a guided meditation with a voice I liked. A friend of mine loves the meditations from a very well-known woman, but I can't stand her voice. Another leading app has the voice of someone who sounds like the guy from Zombies Run! Using that app makes me feel hyper alert to run from zombies! If you try one style and it doesn't work for you, try another one rather than deciding meditation doesn't work for you.

What's excellent about **Calm.com** is that some of the meditations are only two minutes long. That's what I started with—just two minutes a day. There are different meditations for focus, anxiety, creativity, and forgiveness to name only a few. They range from two to 30 minutes. If you feel less than stellar but are unable to sit in the moment for more than a few minutes, put on a two-minute meditation. It's two minutes out of 1,440 in your 24-hour day, but these two minutes can make a world of difference. I meditate daily for about ten minutes first thing in the morning while I'm taking my heart rate variability measurement and before bed to help me relax my brain and sleep. I also do walking meditations in my neighborhood or meditations while traveling and during the day as a transition between tasks or to help me get focused.

If using the term meditation still feels too woo-woo for you, just call it deep breathing. There are a couple of apps, **BreathBuddy** and **Breathe2Relax**, that you can download to focus solely on inhaling and exhaling using the belly. Learning to belly breathe is essential to counteract the shallow chest breathing we tend to do when we're feeling stressed.

These are ideal times for meditation or breathing sessions:

- First thing in the morning to set your intention for the day
- In the evening to wind down
- Between tasks or projects to get focused on the next one
- Between client interactions
- Transitions from home to work and work to home
- Before turning on your computer
- After turning off your computer
- Waiting for the plane to board
- Waiting in line for the train, ride share, or taxi

Meditation takes practice. For most high achievers, it starts out feeling like a waste of time. You sit for two minutes thinking of all the things you could be doing like reacting to email, clicking accept to that meeting invite, checking Facebook, reading the news, or watching TV (heavy on the sarcasm here). Start your session intending to accept what happens. So you think about what you're having for dinner or if your plane will be on time . . . who cares? You're not being graded. Acknowledge the thought and move on. Eventually, you'll be able to focus on the guide or even just your breath. In 2019, I started meditating with a mantra that is my theme word for the year or I practice loving-kindness meditation and focus on sending kindness to myself, a family member, friend or client, and someone I don't know well.

I also use self-hypnosis, which could be considered guided meditation as well. The main difference, according to Barrie St. John at www.selfhypnosis.com, is that hypnosis is "total concentration on a single train of thought." Self-hypnosis has an endgame in mind like sleeping, weight loss, the law of attraction, stopping an unhealthy behavior, etc. The endgame in meditation is to be able to relax the mind and quiet the chatter. I use the **Mindifi** app for sleep hypnosis before bed and when I get up in the middle of the night and can't fall back to sleep quickly. I also use it for health when I'm not feeling my best and law of attraction (the premise that you attract into your universe what you think and experience) when I'm getting ready to perform.

Find something you do every day when traveling or at home and make that your trigger to meditate or practice self-hypnosis. Keep in mind that it's more about practicing consistently than forcing yourself to make it through a long session.

> *After or before (trigger)_____I will practice meditating or self-hypnosis for_____ minutes or breath cycles.*

REFERENCES IN THIS CHAPTER

[1] https://www.sciencemag.org/news/2010/04/multitasking-splits-brain

[2] https://www.apa.org/research/action/multitask

[3] https://nccih.nih.gov/health/228/research

MONTH TEN

PRODUCTIVITY: Boundaries

When I ask workshop participants or private clients if they have a harder time saying yes or saying no, the answer is always it's harder to say no. We feel guilty, unhelpful, afraid of what people will think of us, or maybe we're simply not naturally assertive. After saying yes, we continue to complain about how busy we are and how we never seem to have enough time. Creating boundaries ahead of time helps to take the emotional decision out of whatever we want to do.

Boundaries don't just help us say no, they can also help us say yes to more of the things we truly want. If we want to create boundaries to do more of something, the guidelines might be something like these:

- I will donate X amount of money or time to any charity that involves feeding hungry kids.
- I will go to any play/concert/event that falls on a Saturday night when I am asked.
- I will agree to lead any work project that can be completed within 14 days.

Since most people need boundaries to help them say no, that's what I'll concentrate on, but feel free to change yours as required based on your personality.

Novice: *Charities and Donations*

If I bought every cookie, popcorn, candle, or magazine that my 15 nieces and nephews and friends' kids were selling, I would be broke and have a houseful of stuff I won't use or eat. If I donated my time to every race with a cause, I would never have a Saturday to myself. If I gave money to every non-profit with a mission, I would need a non-profit to pay for me in my old age. I set clear boundaries ahead of time and determine where and how my money and time will be spent so that when I am asked, I have a stock answer (or email) and don't have to think about the decision.

This is what works for my family. Your situation may be different. Feel free to modify my suggestions and templates as they work for you.

Buying "goods" that people are selling for school, church, or clubs: Two of our 15 nieces and nephews are on my side of the family. This makes it easy for me to choose to purchase only from them. There's a caveat because they live in Indiana and we live in North Carolina. They need to create and send us a video selling us the product (the more creative, the better). I will purchase a set amount of the product or if possible, just write a check directly to whatever they are raising money for. This makes it easy to decline when friends' kids or my husband's students ask us to buy something. Since he's a private drum teacher, he could have several students a week asking him to buy things, and he can't play favorites. We simply say that we only buy from two family members, and they have to send a video.

Donating money: At the beginning of the year, my husband and I determine how much money we want to donate to charity. We have supported the Fistula Foundation for about ten years and would prefer to give most of our money to them because it goes to pay for surgeries for women with obstetric fistula. We can make a more significant impact by sending our money to one charity we trust rather than spreading it out over several different charities. We also have a set amount for any type of disaster that may occur so we can donate to the Red Cross or other disaster relief organization.

Since I own a business, I am asked often to donate time or money or to sponsor events. Donating premium coaching time hurts my clients (because it takes time away from when they can schedule with me) and is a money loss for me. Instead, I donate my course, which doesn't cost me anything at this point and is an easy donation. I will give speaking time, but I have one strict criterion which is that people who would invest in hiring me will be in the audience. I know who my clients are and it doesn't make sense for me to give up time speaking if it won't ultimately grow my business.

Having a canned email response to state your charitable boundaries is helpful for both you and your staff because there isn't any question and this removes the emotional decision. After attending one of my workshops, Melinda McKee, the owner of **Memento & Muse**, created the email template following.

Thank you for thinking of Memento & Muse. Unfortunately I'm going to have to pass ~ as a local gifting company we are inundated with donation requests regularly, and in an effort to build a more sustainably responsible giving practice, we now streamline all charitable giving through select hunger relief and food security causes. Hope you understand! Wishing you the very best of luck on this project.

As a former chair of the Events Committee for a non-profit, I had the job of soliciting donations and was really proud of her when I received this back! It clearly states her boundaries and that she does donate but only to specific types of organizations. I didn't feel insulted because mine didn't fit into her criteria. Beautiful!

My company donates a percentage of proceeds to **Kiva.org**. Kiva is a microlending site that helps people from all over the world in special projects by crowdsourcing money to lend them. They then have to pay back the money over time. That money goes back into my Kiva funds, and I can choose whether to reinvest. My assistant Rea is from the Philippines, so we choose a woman from that country every time we have money to give. I also use it as a business growth and teaching opportunity. We decide on a woman based on her length of time in business, specific situation, and the likelihood of getting paid back. It's been a gratifying way to bond with Rea over helping women in her country.

*Helping can be a self-reward too. The best thing about our Kiva project is I am included in the decision. It is even more special because we dedicate each donation to the people in my country. This inspires me and helps me realize that rewarding yourself by helping others is more fulfilling.— **Rea Donato, Happiness Specialist, Work Well. Play More!***

As far as time goes, choose how many hours or events you will donate to at the beginning of the year. Create a time donation budget and keep track. If you hit that budget, you can reply back or state that you have allowed yourself a specific number of volunteer hours this year and you have met that budget. They can check back with you next year. This tells them that you *do* volunteer your time but that you allocate it wisely. If they want you next year, they'll need to ask well in advance.

I am on a couple of boards and councils, serve as a mentor, and get asked to serve in other ways at least quarterly. I limit myself to a specific number of boards and committees and won't join another unless I roll off of one of my current board commitments. This means it has to be a *hell yes* for me to do it. If I can't fully commit to something, it doesn't do them any good to have me participate. I don't want to be a warm body and would rather be narrow and deep in whatever I'm involved in than wide and shallow, giving a little to a lot but not really making a significant difference.

If you are part of a company with colleagues who actively participate in races, charities, and other events, consider donating smaller amounts or deciding as a team what is respectful.

> *I will donate $ _____, _____hours, and serve on no more than _____ committees or boards. I will reevaluate quarterly or yearly, depending on my situation. I will create a prepared response to decline or explain requests so that I can eliminate the emotional decision at the moment.*

Pro: *Personal*

Personal boundaries are where the majority of my clients struggle—play dates, invitations to parties, requests to attend social events. It all becomes too much, and we fill our evenings and weekends with so much activity, we don't feel like we ever get a breath and always feel behind. I'm an extrovert, but I need a lot of privacy. I have no problem saying no and never experience FOMO or Fear Of Missing Out when it comes to social engagements. I stick with the JOOO—Joy Of Opting Out—because sometimes the joy is spending an afternoon on a Sunday reading and painting my nails. I might miss something fun every once in a while but regret fewer things I say no to than when I used to always say yes, and regret that I wasn't relaxing or catching up on other things.

Remember, every time you say *yes* you are saying *no* to something else.

I have a lot of friends, but the ones that are in my Tier One (admit it, you have tiers too) are always a priority. I schedule my next date with them while we are still in our current one. This way, I'm not giving up my calendar before prioritizing the people I love the most.

I frequently travel for work, so I don't give up my time easily when I'm home. I use the *Hell Yes* method and ask myself, is this a *Hell yes I want to go*? If it is not, the default answer is no. Derek Sivers' 3-minute YouTube video is good encouragement to saying no: **https://www.youtube.com/watch?v=1ehWlVeMrqw**

When I have a fully-packed month and get an invitation, if

it's not a "hell yes" for me, then I respond with something like, "My schedule is already full this month and I'm choosing not to add anything else." Or "I'm in a time of high-priority and only doing mission-critical events and tasks." Or "My schedule is full this month, so I'm only doing activities that also involve my husband Kevin." During the time between Thanksgiving and New Year's Day, when I have more parties than I could possibly attend, I choose only the most critical or "hell yes!" parties and the rest I decline. Saying no takes practice.

> *I will schedule time each month in order of priority—private, spouse, family, Tier One friends, and other (whatever your preference would be). I will consider each invitation and determine 1) is this a "hell, yes?" or 2) is it worth saying no to have (time alone, time with family, etc.)*

Master: Work

Your ability to set boundaries at work may depend mainly on your job role. One thing to focus on is your time. Do you allow people to interrupt you all day? Set boundaries by making it clear when you need GSD focus time (without abusing it) and sticking to those times. If you say that every morning you would like uninterrupted time from nine to ten thirty but then you go and disrupt other people or allow others to interrupt you, you are training your team that you can be interrupted. If you use a door hanger or other visible sign, then use it during your focus time and take it off when you are done.

Set boundaries for email, phone, or text communication during your off-hours. If you make the decision that you want a separation between work and home, don't answer texts, emails, or phone calls during those hours. The first time you do, you have trained people that you work during those times. Only deviate during planned events like project launches or when someone needs back-up.

If you want to leave at a particular time each day, keep a strict schedule and create a boundary around the clock. No one questions the parents who have to leave the office at four to pick their child up from daycare, yet people without children tend to get asked frequently or dumped on for the later work. I knew a guy who told his office for a year that he had a dog at home that he had to let out and walk, so he left at 5:15 exactly. This man had no pets, but he did get to his spin class every night without guilt or being given a hard time.

I had a client who felt terrible about leaving at a reasonable hour. She would often stay late and then get home starving and resort to processed, microwaveable meals. She was planning a trip to Italy and needed to get in shape by walking after she got home each night. She made a game out of needing to leave at six so she could pick up "Italy" at the bus stop. This was a reminder to her that if she were a parent, she would not let her kid stand outside waiting for her. She would leave and take care of her responsibilities—in this case, her health.

If you are asked to take on additional projects or work on top of an already-packed workload and don't know how to fit it in, ask your manager what your priorities should be and what can either be dropped or given less attention. This is import-ant. We all take on additional responsibilities sometimes, but setting expectations up front is imperative for both you and your manager.

> *I will choose a work boundary related to my schedule, focus time, or additional projects and create and communicate those guidelines.*

DECLUTTER: Storage Areas

Ah, yeah, here's a big one. This one might take a weekend or two and a few weekends to get geared up to do it. Whatever your process, let's kick it into high gear. If you really want to become an Olympic-level declutterer, try using this section once a quarter or at the end of each season. You'll keep those main storage areas clutter-free and organized, which will make getting to all activities with the right equipment so much easier. Your future self will thank your present self for implementing these changes.

Novice: Hazardous Materials

Hazardous materials sit around our house and storage areas because they aren't easy to get rid of for a good reason. They also aren't useful to keep around our houses if we aren't using them. Hazardous materials include paint, varnish, toxic cleaners, pesticides, motor oil, etc. Most communities have hazardous waste days where people can drop off products at a specific location or leave them out for pick-up during their regular trash day. Check your city's guidelines for proper disposal. Other websites to review are **https://www. epa.gov/hw/household-hazardous-waste-hhw** and **https:// www.moving.com/tips/how-to-dispose-of-hazardous-wast e-before-you-move/**.

It's unfortunate that municipalities make it so difficult when people try to do the right thing. One friend of mine called two pharmacies and a police department to find out how to destroy used epi-pens and not one of them could tell her how. I know this is a challenge and trust me, I feel your pain, but two times a year let's suck it up and do it.

So—why *are* you hanging on to that jug of car window cleaner and moving it to three different houses when you get your window cleaner replenished at the auto shop? (Okay, this was me.) Why are you keeping a bag full of old batteries or all your burned-out lightbulbs? (Same!) Because it is a pain to dispose of them—but this month, we are trying to do it the right way and remove these hazardous materials from our homes.

> *I will properly dispose of or recycle all hazardous materials twice yearly in March and August (or whatever dates you prefer).*

Pro: *Sports or Hobby Equipment*

When I competed in adventure racing and triathlons, I eventually had six different bikes, loads of equipment, and my garage looked like a sporting goods store. When I decided to retire, it took about a year, but I sold all but two mountain bikes and still have those plus my spin and Fitbike. For me, this is minimal, and yes, I use each one.

Is your sporting or hobby equipment just an unused reminder of the past? If you want to get back to using it, set up a plan to get back in the game. If you don't want to use it anymore, donate or sell it to someone who will, especially if it makes you feel like a failure or that you *should* be using it.

With some things, bikes included, if you wait too long to sell, your ability to make money will decrease as new technology or styles hit the stores. Let someone else honor your equipment. I had a family member who inherited her dad's tools. Neither she nor her husband used them, and they sat in her garage for years. Sadly, by the time she decided to get rid of them, not only could she not sell them, she couldn't even donate them to a local school because they were so outdated. In another situation, a former client gave her father's wood working tools to my husband, and he has used them to create beautiful bowls and boxes to give away and to sell.

> *I will purge my unused sports or hobby equipment to sell or donate to someone who will actually use it.*

Master: *Garage, Basement, Attic, or Shed*

Everyone has an area at home that is a receptacle for stuff. Even if you don't have a garage, basement, attic, shed, or storage unit, (and if you have a storage unit, try explaining that American concept to your Filipino Virtual Assistant), you probably have a closet, spare bedroom, or crawl space. It's not going to get any easier. Pick a few days this month, or even a few hours if it's overwhelming, and start with the easy stuff, getting rid of broken junk you thought you might one day get around to fixing, stuff you don't use, and trash or items that are outdated.

Where I live in Raleigh, there seem to be storage unit facilities popping up every other week. What a racket! People put things in storage for months or even years and pay the monthly fee thinking someday they will go through their stuff. Really? If you haven't needed it in a year, then you can get rid of it. If you have a storage unit and it's so overwhelming you can't bear to go through it alone, hire a professional organizer to go through it with you. The money you will spend on a professional to help you clean it out will save you money in storage unit fees.

My husband and I cleaned out our shed and garage using the KonMarie method. It took a couple of weekends, but every time I open the door to either one, it makes me feel happy. Now we have a date to do a quick declutter every quarter to make sure it doesn't get out of hand.

Overwhelmed? Hire a professional garage organizer (yes, they exist!). Remember, you can even just hit one bin, basket, or box, and I'll accept it for this month. But maybe you do that every month!

Sane Jane Professional Organizing (Raleigh, NC) was AMAZING! Well worth the investment. And the best part? I gave her full permission to toss anything she saw as junk. It was much easier to outsource the physical throwing away to someone else who didn't have any emotional attachment. And she was great about pushing back on things that I almost held onto . . . like 3 buckets of the kids' beach seashells! — **Sylvia Inks**

> *I will do a decluttering session for my _____, my most cluttered area, in a way that doesn't make me feel overwhelmed.*

HEALTH: Screen-Free Meals

I grew up eating in front of a TV. The kitchen table was reserved for holidays when people were visiting, but even then, the TV was still on. We had TV trays and they were our tables. Now I can't stand to eat a meal in front of the TV. It happens occasionally, but it feels like an insult to whatever it is that I prepared. One of the shifts for me nine years ago was when our house moved to Netflix-only. Since I had to be intentional about what I wanted to watch, it seemed silly to turn it on and then go sit at the table.

At home, I eat at the table, the bar, or on my screened-in porch, even when I'm by myself. I'm not entirely mindful though (perfectly imperfect). I *do* eat my smoothie bowl breakfast while working because I want to get right to work in the morning. I can stretch out the smoothie forty-five minutes to an hour and sitting and eating a smoothie while doing nothing else seems well—weird. But on *most* days, no matter how fully packed I am, I will take ten minutes to go and sit and have my lunch or dinner away from my computer. Taking even that short time away helps me reboot and allows my mind to rest. I can enjoy my meal more and feel more satisfied later in the day.

A consistent theme among my beta readers when they read this chapter is how much eating at a table as a family impacted their lives. All said it made them feel more connected and was a way to be engaged with their family, partner, or roommate in today's hectic world.

Novice: Screen-Free Lunch

Substitute *device for TV*—laptop, computer, tablet, or phone—and many of us still eat in front of a screen. There is even a hashtag *#SadDeskLunch*.

- Brian Wansink of **Mindless Eating** found that people consumed approximately 30 percent more calories later in the day if they ate lunch at their desks while working.

That can really add up over the year and lead to afternoon munchies. If we are staring at the screen while we eat, it doesn't get imprinted on our brain that we have eaten, and we aren't as satisfied. In fact, one of the three best ways to boost your productivity in the afternoon is to eat lunch away from your desk. Your brain needs that recovery time, so if you don't take that break, you are saying goodbye to an inspired afternoon or evening.

Screen-free can also save your life! I almost ate one of those oxygen absorber packages from a bag of beef jerky because I was multitasking and not paying attention. (I'm not kidding!) Okay, it might not have killed me, but it definitely made me think harder about what I was putting in my mouth!

Lunch is for wimps.— *Gordon Gekko, Wall Street (rated one of the Top 50 movie villains of all time)*

Eating lunch away from your desk will also force you to get up off of your butt and help prevent glute amnesia. You can connect with another co-worker or just use the time to eat and thinkitate.

- The Hartman Group **https://www.hartman-group.com/** found that 62 percent of professionals eat lunch at their desks.

We feel like eating lunch at our desk is going to save us time from working at home later that day or that we can get caught up, but the law of diminishing returns shows that it doesn't actually make us any more efficient.

Most people would assume that the staff at the Nantahala Outdoor Center have plenty of opportunities to eat away from their desks and enjoy eating outside in the beautiful mountain and river surroundings. However, many of them were the victims of #SadDeskLunches. A couple of weeks after I gave a workshop on productivity behaviors, the CEO sent me a screenshot of a Facebook message from Lindsey Alexandra to the staff that said:

Wesser Lunch Bunch on Wednesdays @ Noon

Come get away from your desk and work. Eat your lunch and get to know some of your amazing co-workers while enjoying some time by the river. #NoMoreSadDeskLunches

That made my week! Sometimes it takes a leader to make it acceptable to get away from your desk. Be that leader.

I'm going to be realistic here and not pretend that you are going to go from five days of eating at your desk to none, so let's try for one screen-free lunch each week. Maybe in a few weeks, your goal will be to have three screen-free lunches.

> *I will eat a screen-free (no devices or reading material) meal at work ___ times per week away from my desk and will enjoy it by myself or with other people or I will eat a screen-free meal on these days every week _____.*

Pro: Screen-Free Meal Day

Now that you have implemented screen-free meals at work, how about having at least one day a week that you eat *all* your meals screen free? For me, I don't eat any meals on Sunday in front of a screen because my one meal a day where I usually eat in front of a screen (breakfast) isn't a smoothie and it's with my husband. It's a reminder that food isn't just fuel. It's something to be enjoyed and appreciated.

> *I will eat all meals _____ days per week screen-free or I will eat screen-free meals every _____ (day of the week).*

Master: *Mindful Meal*

Now that you've had practice eating meals without a screen, how about trying a mindful meal? Even if we aren't looking at a device, we might still be distracted and not fully thinking about what we are putting in our mouths. Mindful eating means smelling, tasting, and chewing your food, not just shoveling it into your mouth. It means putting the utensil down between bites and really savoring the meal. It's a practice in patience and gratitude. Because this makes you eat more slowly you may find that you eat less. As I mentioned earlier, I eat my food with chopsticks as much as I can because it makes me take my time. I have a travel set I keep in my purse. I also eat from tiny demitasse spoons to take smaller bites.

If you decide to try eating a mindful meal, why not make it a full-blown ritual? Use pretty dishes, sit in a quiet place, light a candle, or play some uplifting music if it helps you set the mood. Close your eyes for some of your bites and chew the food thoroughly before you swallow it. I find this is best done alone, and I'll do this after a particularly busy day or while I am held captive on a plane.

I will practice mindful eating _____ times per week or during these meals _____ on these days _____.

MONTH ELEVEN

PRODUCTIVITY: Outsourcing

I firmly believe in outsourcing the things you don't like doing when you can afford to do that. There are so many ways to outsource that will free up your time, save money in the long run, and you don't have to be fancy or rich to do it. The first thing to consider is how much your time is worth. Of course, this is an estimate because money is never worth as much as time. You can always make more money, but you can't make more time.

Not sure how to calculate how much your time is worth? There are a couple of different ways to do it. The easiest way is to determine how much you want to make this year or how much you currently make per year. Divide that by the number of weeks per year you work. Divide again by the number of hours you want to work per week = Bingo. This is how much your time is worth. If you're worth $96 per hour, then hiring a VA for $30 per hour for eight hours a month will let you focus your time on what matters most and save you money in the long run.

I also recommend using the Personal Earnings Goal or PEG method to determine how much it costs you or your family to live per hour. I've included the website link in the bonus chapter. This takes a little more time, but it helped me determine how much I need to make to live, my yearly goals for my business, and what type of assistant was vital for me.

Novice: *Subscribe to Set and Forget*

I *love* Amazon Subscribe and Save, and if you are a Prime member, it's a crime not to use this set-it-and-forget-it option. If you aren't a Prime Member, the $119 you spend a year will blow your Costco, Sam's Club, and BJ's membership out of the water. You get free, expedited shipping, access to movies and music streaming, one free Kindle book a month, and 10 percent off select Whole Foods items. With Amazon S&S, you can place orders for items ranging from groceries to batteries, skin-care products to socks. Your order is delivered on a flexible schedule that you choose—monthly, every three months, every six months, etc.—which can also be changed by moving up or skipping a month. I buy almost all my dry goods, paper products, makeup—anything I would go to Target or Wal-Mart to purchase—on Amazon S&S. If you have more than five things in the order, you get 15 percent off the already low price.

There are many other subscription services including **Thrive Market** and **Green Polka Dot Box** that can deliver groceries to your door. I'm a recent devotee of **Brandless**. It's based out of California and has direct relationships with suppliers to be able to eliminate the extra costs for unnecessary markups. You don't know what the brand is because, as the name suggests, it's brandless, but I've scanned a barcode and it has popped up as a brand I would pay at least 50 percent more for in stores. I get my household cleaners, some beauty and personal care products, and pantry goods from them. All of their food is non-GMO, and they don't allow animal testing on personal products.

Think you can't afford a personal shopper? Think again. My clients have had mad success with clothing delivery services (Refer to Month Five's Declutter habit). After setting preferences, getting very specific with style and size and picking out looks that you like from the site, these services deliver a box to your door every month or quarter with clothing curated uniquely for you. Some services are for purchase only and need to be returned within seventy-two hours, and others are more like rentals where you receive a new shipment when they receive your returns. I like the clothing rental subscriptions because I don't want to be photographed in the same outfit more than once when I speak. It also cuts down on my dry-cleaning expenses because I don't have to clean the clothes before I send them back.

These types of services are ideal for people who aren't stylish, don't like to shop, don't have time to buy, or just want to break out of their comfort zones. Two of my clients have been shocked at how well the clothes fit and how much having new outfits "on demand" made them feel like a walking magazine cover. When you look good, you feel good. When you feel good, you take better care of yourself and have more confidence. A list of men's and women's clothing delivery services can be found in the bonus chapter.

I also sell and buy clothes from **thredUP**, which has gently used clothing or new with tags. The prices are unreal, I can filter easily so I don't get overwhelmed, and they have a generous return policy if something doesn't fit.

> *At 5'1", I'm limited to petite size clothing and it stinks to have to try on 12 items to get a good fit. My Stitch Fix arrives every three months with five pieces for me to choose from. I can buy one or none. It allows me to avoid the mall, big messy department stores and keeps me out of a fashion rut because my stylist sends me items I may not have otherwise picked out, but end up loving. I use Rockbox and pay a monthly rental of $21 for trendy jewelry that I can wear a few times and send back, or buy the pieces I love at a discount. This keeps me fashion forward because I'm always wearing at least one trendy item that pairs well with my classic pieces.*— **Lilly Ferrick, Sales Growth Partner**

Birch Box is a beauty and grooming subscription that surprises you each month with supplies like makeup, shaving accessories, and shampoo and comes in both men's and women's boxes. I subscribe to **Dollar Shave Club** and get blades delivered to my door on a set schedule. It is way cheaper than retail, the quality is excellent, and their marketing is hilarious. These types of subscription services also make great gifts.

> *I will try one subscription service to save me time, energy, decisions, and/or money.*

Pro: *Personal Outsourcing*

Personal assistants (PAs) can sometimes overlap with virtual assistants and house assistant services. Some people feel embarrassed about hiring a personal or house assistant. Either they think that only wealthy people use them or that they *should* be able to get the tasks done themselves. If this is what you're thinking, go back to the question, "how much is your time worth?" Would you rather be catching up on errands and chores or going to the TEDx event or playing in your club softball game? Besides, you are giving someone a job and in the case of my house assistant, allowing her to work in her line of genius, which involves serving others. Your company may have an agreement with a concierge service and provide a discounted rate. Check with your benefits department first.

Concierge and personal assistant services include tasks such as:

- Laundry and ironing
- Light or detailed cleaning
- Running errands such as grocery shopping, shipping/mailing, dry cleaning drop off/pick up
- Food prep
- Accepting home deliveries or meeting workers to do home maintenance services
- Performing research
- Managing vehicle maintenance
- Managing household projects
- Help with party planning and hosting services
- Light gardening or yard work
- Serving as a house manager

By using a website like **www.care.com** or **www.taskrabbit. com** you can put all your specific requirements in a job posting and even do background checks on the people who respond to your request.

I've written about my house assistant several times on my blog, and I would sacrifice whatever I needed to keep her. She comes once per week for four or five hours and chops and preps all the food from my Community Supported Agriculture box, folds and puts away my laundry, cleans the bathroom and kitchen, and, if she has time, cleans the rest of the house. She sews, mends, and runs errands if I need her to. I call her a house assistant, but she's more like a house angel. My clients who have hired an assistant to pick up and put away groceries, prepare meals, and run errands also don't know what they ever did without them.

If you travel a lot, this is the number one outsourcing service I recommend. When you are traveling the last thing you want to do when you are home is chores. It may also eliminate the arguments about who should be cleaning—the one who is home making a mess or the one traveling because they aren't participating in the other household tasks. If your relationship with your partner or roommate is in trouble over chores, the first thing to do is hire a housecleaner to come in as often as you would like. Once weekly or once monthly works for most. At the very least, arrange for someone to come in quarterly for deep cleaning. I consider housecleaning cheaper than marriage therapy and am not at all shy about using my house assistant since my husband and I have different standards and timelines. The same goes for two working parents. Outsource and spend the time feeling positive about each other instead of mentally keeping track and feeling resentful if you are the primary tasker. Single? You deserve it too because all of the responsibilities are yours!

> *I love my home assistant! She is a combination of a housekeeper and a personal assistant. My HA takes care of many other things for me in addition to cleaning, like washing the dust ruffle on my bed, keeping my linen closet clean and organized, doing the laundry, and watering the plants. Because one of her duties is to clean the patio furniture, my husband and I can enjoy each other's company together on our porch during summer nights. All this, so I can focus on my business during the day and enjoy our home and my husband when I'm not working.* — *Lilly Ferrick, Sales Growth Partner*

If you don't like doing your laundry, don't have time to do it, or don't have a washer and dryer in your residence, in which case the time to do laundry can be extra costly, consider dropping off your laundry twice monthly at a local laundromat. Make it a line item in your budget. The bonus is that your clothes won't be delivered with all the wrinkles you have from doing them on your own, stuffing them back in the bag to tote home, or leaving them in the dryer.

When we bought our second home, we were on .2 of an acre. We thought it was a step up. It didn't take long for us to realize that we liked the idea of having a yard but neither of us wanted to do the work to make it look nice. Then we moved to a townhome and had landscapers included in our HOA fee. I could enjoy my yard with the occasional planting of a flower or two. Now we live on an acre and my husband mows again, but it isn't as daunting because we have more trees than grass. General lawn care can be cheap. If you are getting warning letters from the city saying your grass is too high or you just don't want to be mowing in 100 degrees in July—outsource.

For one-off tasks, consider a service like **TaskRabbit**, which is offered in several major cities. It's full of freelancers who will do handyperson tasks, moving and packing, furniture assembly, wrap gifts, put up and take down your holiday decorations—the options could be endless. If it's been on your list for a long time, give someone a job and pay for it to be done.

> *I will outsource this task that I don't like doing, am not good at, or have been procrastinating doing:* _____.

Master: *Professional Outsourcing*

Virtual assistants can do every kind of office task you can imagine including scheduling, answering email, customer service, email campaigns, travel arrangements, and social media. The list goes on depending on what type of VA you hire. There are many services like **Fancy Hands, Ruby Receptionist, Virtual Staff Finder,** and **Get Friday.** Some companies are set up to be task-oriented meaning you pay for a specific number of tasks per month and any VA could be assigned to do that task. For example, plans with Fancy Hands are by task instead of by the hour. You don't get a dedicated VA this way, but paying per job can sometimes work in your favor. Don't have time to be on hold for 20 minutes with tech support? Fancy Hands will hold for you and patch you in when they join. Need to do some research for your summer vacay? Get Friday can research it for you.

Other services give you a dedicated VA and bill you for a set number of hours per month. You also may have a local virtual assistant who works from home but can pick up marketing materials at a printer and deliver them to a venue or run your business errands for instance. Using an hourly VA or VA service helps budget your money because you don't have to employ them all year, and you may be able to change your hourly needs each month depending on the service. There are options for every need and budget.

Overwhelmed and need a VA but don't know where to start or how to use one? First, write down everything you do daily that is personal and work-related. This may take some time and works best throughout a week or even a month, since some time suckers aren't done daily. Next, look carefully at that list. If you consider what you earn per hour, how much money are you wasting doing tasks you could be outsourcing? Are you doing $10/hour tasks when your time is worth $50 or more? My guess is you are. Why? Because these are usually tasks like scheduling, social media posts, researching flights, etc. that make us feel good to tick off the list but aren't revenue producing and often take more time than we realize.

Track your time to find out how long you are spending on $10/hour tasks and assign those first. *Note that virtual assistants cost more than $10/hour.* I use that term to make a point. There are tasks you shouldn't be doing because they aren't in your line of genius. Consider the type of assistant you need. Do you need admin work? Travel arrangements? Scheduling? Hire a virtual assistant. Need help with social media? Hire a digital assistant. Want someone to grocery shop, run errands, and chop your vegetables? Hire a personal assistant.

After you've decided what tasks to assign, start writing down precise instructions for each job, or better yet, record yourself doing them online using a program like **Zoom, Jing,** or **Screencast.**

If you know someone who uses a VA, get a referral or recommendation. Many people opt to go the cheap route and hire a student, intern, friend, or family member. Know that many VAs have owned their own businesses or have business degrees and are very experienced and skilled. They choose to work from home and make their own hours, so they opt for a VA position. Sometimes you get what you pay for and if you want to pay minimum wage, you might get someone you will end up spending two to three times as long teaching to do your tasks only to have them quit in a few weeks. Interns and students always seem like a great option to frugal folks, but keep in mind that they will only be with you a few months and then you will have to do the interview and training part all over again. Also hiring students or interns should be considered an altruistic opportunity because you need to provide training and real-life skills to them, not just dump work on them without spending time mentoring.

I hired Mel, my virtual assistant, because I was swamped with tasks like searching for images and hunting down Call for Speakers links for specific conferences. These tasks are critical for my business, but they sucked up my time. I worked with Marcey to identify the functions that made the most sense to outsource and what skills were needed to complete those tasks. I was reluctant to hire a VA full-time because of the financial risk, so I piloted working with Mel half-time for 3 months. After those 3 months, I hired him full-time. Now he does image searches and designs graphics for me, saving me precious

time to work in my line of genius. — Wendy Gates Corbett,
Professional Speaker and Founder of Refresher
Training

I hired my virtual assistant through **Virtual Staff Finders** in the Philippines. They are a recruitment service that finds up to five people that fit your needs for you to interview. When you hire them, they are your employee or contractor, and you pay them directly. I've had Rea full-time for four years, and she is fantastic. I've also steered clients to Virtual Staff Finders as well, and they have had excellent results. My VA has a degree in IT, creates all my marketing materials, has built all four of my websites, and has built client sites as well. She is much more than an administrative assistant but will still do those tasks too. I've never met her in person, but I trust her completely. We plan to meet face-to-face in 2020 to mark our five years of working together.

I've used **Fiverr** for book formatting and the cover design of my first book, graphics, and press releases. If there is a task to be done, there is someone on Fiverr willing to do it. Some jobs do cost $5 per task (or gig in Fiverr-speak), but many freelancers worth hiring on Fiverr charge multiple gigs for one task. It's helpful to get recommendations and always look at the reviews and ratings for each person. Need to do market research? Hire someone from Fiverr instead. Want to compile a collage or video of your family holiday photos? Take your pick. One client had her entire website done for $30 and it looks fantastic. I used Fiverr to have a "celebrity" send my husband a special 50th birthday message and to take my niece's photo and turn her into a cartoon Rapunzel.

> *I will test a virtual assistant service, Upwork, or Fiverr for a task I've wanted to take off of my plate that isn't in my line of genius.*

DECLUTTER: Sentimental Items

Getting rid of sentimental items can spark a whirlwind of emotions in some people. Even discussing it can cause anger, tears, and frustration among family members whose feelings get hurt or insulted that you don't want Grandma's cookbook holder when you don't cook or Uncle Daryl's toolset that you don't have room for. The level of sentiment can vary among age groups (Matures and Boomers tend to want to keep sentimental items more than Gen Xers and Millennials) and also among types of homes (if you have a basement, attic, and/or garage, you are more likely to be able to store the item than someone in an apartment).

I am a thoughtful person, but I don't attach a lot of feeling to items. I don't allow my family to guilt me into thinking something should be meaningful. If it's going to sit in a box somewhere on a shelf, it's not serving as a sweet reminder of someone anyway. I never want an object to feel like a burden that turns into resentment. If you are a person who tends to hang onto a lot of sentimental items, is it more out of guilt or because you really want whatever it is you have and it sparks a warm memory?

When my grandma passed away, I was asked if I wanted several of her things, but all I wanted was her Scrabble board because we played the game together my entire life. It is a great memory, and it's also useful. I kept my grandpa's cane. It hangs on my wall where I can see it. It makes me think of him daily.

Novice: Photos

Photos are one of the easiest things to purge yet the hardest for some people to get rid of. I think this will be less of an issue in the future since we store them digitally now instead of printing them. If you have a box of photos that you never look at, you could snap pictures of them with your phone or have them all scanned and stored in the cloud where you actually might look at them occasionally. This is a great Taskrabbit task or trusted-college-student-home-on-a-break task! When was the last time you pulled that box out from under the bed?

If you still don't feel right about throwing photos away, ask yourself these questions for the first round of purging:

- Do I know who all the people are in this picture?

- Is the photo good quality?

- Does everyone look good and would they all want this photo displayed?

- Would I pay to have this photo printed?

- Is this my only copy of the photo?

For me, if the answer to any of the questions is no, then I toss the photo. I don't want some low-quality photo where I have one eye crossed, am sitting or standing with poor posture, and am wearing ill-fitting shorts to be in rotation (unless it was Halloween and on purpose!).

Another thing to consider is a fire or flood. My friend Sara lost all of her best of photos from her twenties and early thirties due to flooding from a hurricane. If photos are that important, have them scanned.

> *I will toss photos that don't spark a fond memory or aren't regularly looked at.*

Pro: *Joy-Suckers?*

Are you keeping items that make you feel depressed, lonely, sad, or angry? What is the point of keeping the letters from your ex-boyfriend who dumped you unceremoniously before the big event? What about that sweater that your aunt bought you that was two sizes too small so you could "shrink" into it. I had a book from a family member and felt guilty for years about wanting to throw it away. There were so many mixed feelings when I looked at that book—guilt, frustration, stupidity—that when I finally got rid of it, I was relieved and wondered why I waited so long. No one was stressing about it but me, and it definitely wasn't worth it. In Marie Kondo's language, if it doesn't spark joy . . . bye-bye!

> *I will get rid of all sentimental items that are sucking my joy.*

Master: One Box

Erin Doland, author of *Unclutter Your Life in One Week*, advocates that each family member have one box for sentimental items. I love this approach because it encourages me to be selective and choose what really is meaningful for me. If I want to add something to the box and it's full, I need to take something out. That's usually no problem. What might have been significant for me five years ago may not be now. What's even more important, though, is giving my family the one box rule. Many of us have guilt about throwing away loved one's items when they die. In my Will, I have stated explicitly that each family member can have one box (or less) of whatever they want and what is left can be thrown away or donated without guilt (yes, I used those words). This takes the pressure off and gives them permission to do what is best for them. I don't want to be cluttering up people's homes in my afterlife.

> **I will purge sentimental items down to one box or bin.**

HEALTH: Mindset

Clutter isn't just physical or digital. It's also mental. We all have some head trash that is probably taking up space in our brains and not serving us well. Using specific words or changing the way we think about ourselves or the situations we are in can create a massive shift in our behavior and attitude.

Novice: Busy Is a Choice

Have you ever made yourself busier than you need to be and somehow got satisfaction out of saying how busy you were? Why do people do this? Shouldn't we want to be productive so we can spend our time enjoying our lives and playing more? We wear *Busy* like a badge. I can be busy all day searching the web and calling it research. But this isn't productive or useful. I know a woman who is always talking about how busy her life is. She's been busy for 25 years, no matter what job she has, the season of the year, or whether her kids are at home or grown and married. I think she gets something out of it—some sort of payoff—because she fills her day up with trivial tasks and then complains about her lack of time. Do you see yourself in here somewhere? I try not to use the word busy and will correct myself and others when they refer to my schedule that way. It's my four-letter word. *Busy is a choice.*

Stop being busy and start working! People become martyrs and braggarts about how busy they are. I have heard people take their voices down to a whisper to tell me they only work about 35 to 40 hours per week either because they feel guilty or they know that more work will get piled on them. It's too bad salaried people don't get incentivized for being efficient. One reason I didn't tell my former manager right away about how much time I was saving by processing email and working offline was that I was afraid I would just get more work added to my already full load. Sometimes being productive can feel like a punishment. On the other hand, you could say, "I improved my efficiency by working this way, and now I'm able to take on a new project to further my career!"

Work on your business, not your busyness. — **Tatyana Blankenship, Certified Project Manager**

Our society has a pervasive addiction to being busy. We have forgotten how to sit and be still and present. We can't stand in line or wait for the elevator to go up for 12 seconds without looking at our phones. We must always be *doing*. I am as guilty as anyone and feel like I should try to be productive everywhere and at all times; however, sometimes taking that mental break is what makes me *more* productive.

I conducted a workshop at an organization where participants couldn't stop talking about how beautiful their office building was and how there was a path outside to walk. The funny thing is that no one ever took advantage of that path because they felt if they were seen walking outside, people would think they should be working. If they spoke about how busy or overloaded they were, people would remember that they were away from their desks out on a walk! Since I was working with the entire group, I told them to reframe those thoughts and look at those people out walking on the path as renewing their productivity and energy muscles. The lazy brains and butts were the ones sitting at their desks all day.

At another one of my workshops, someone asked me how to respond when they really are fully scheduled and don't want to take on any more work, responsibilities, or go to that play-date or party on the weekend.

When my calendar is full, instead of saying "I'm too busy," I will respond with something like this (see also Month Ten, Productivity, Pro: Personal):

"My calendar is full right now and I'm only adding in mission-critical opportunities."

"I have a lot going on this month and any free time is going to be focused on my husband/resting/me-time, etc."

"This month is full, but if you would like to suggest something next month (or holiday, or quarter), I can look for time in my schedule."

"If I fit anything else into my schedule, I won't be able to fully commit, and I don't do things half-assed."

I've never had anyone push back and, in fact, have had people 1) tell me they appreciated my honesty or 2) say they respected that I have boundaries.

> *I will use a different adjective to describe my schedule or time. I will refrain from using the word "busy" because it's boring and it's a choice.*

Pro: Stop Should-ing All Over Yourself

I should exercise more.
I should eat more vegetables.
I should call my prospects.
I should call my mom/dad more.
I should read more books.
I should . . . I should . . . until I should all over myself.

Read that out loud for maximum impact.

"Should" is another word I don't often use. When I do, it's an accident and I will go back and substitute something else. "Should" implies *failure*. We have failed at something or are somehow not fulfilling our obligations. It never makes us feel good. Instead, use *I will, I want to,* or *I get to.*

One of my clients doesn't like to call his mother. She's in assisted living, and she spends most of the call complaining about how bad the food is, her different aches and pains, and the latest death among the people she knows. He said it never makes him feel good when he gets off the phone, but he knows he needs to call her. She's his mother and talking to her son makes her happy. He can't use the word "want" because he really doesn't want to, but he *will.* It's not a failure, it's a fact. He will call his mother on Sundays.

A workshop attendee said to me, "I have four kids under the age of five and I really should go on a date with my wife every month." I asked him if he wanted to and he said, "Absolutely." I asked him to change his language and for his wife to do the same. About six months later, he sent an email saying how vital that subtle change was. When they started saying they wanted to, it was present or future tense instead of focusing on the failure of the past. They ended up feeling like it was their mission because they wanted to and went out more in those six months than they had in two years.

Another workshop attendee said he used the words *get to.* He gets to wash the dishes every night. After a few chuckles in the room, he said, "My wife makes dinner every night. I get to do the dishes because my wife makes a meal for us. I don't have to resort to fast food or worry about what I'm going to eat. We both work, and she gets to cook dinner and I get to clean up." Now that's a healthy mindset!

> *I will not should on myself. Where I would have naturally used that word in the past, I will replace it with I will, I want, or I get to.*

Master: *Accountability and Coaching*

I'm putting accountability and coaching under mindset because both can have a significant impact on our mindsets. Some people don't like the word accountability. They feel insulted that they need it. To them it means they don't have discipline or they have failed. I used to feel this way until I shifted it to indicate support. I didn't even really know what a coach was until I started my business. The only coaches I had been exposed to were sports coaches and a life coach I had used several years prior. Now I am dedicated to the coaching process and not just because I am one. I have had different coaches at various stages in my business and would definitely not be where I am today in my career or my life had I not found my support system. I've had coaches help me with mindset, marketing, determining my ideal client, relationships with my staff, self-worth, image, valuing my services, and professional speaking.

We all have things we don't like doing or procrastinate doing and could use support to get done. Sometimes, just having someone to be accountable to helps us be intentional and map out a plan to reach our goals. No matter what, it always starts with you. Your partner or team will hold you responsible, but you're the one who has to do the work.

I was in an accountability group with my friend Lilly and my brother Todd while we were completing a round of **The Freedom Journal**. The Freedom Journal is intense, so it helped to have other people going through it. We all had a numbers goal that we were trying to achieve in our businesses. We met every other week, and we would text each other every time we got a hot prospect or closed a deal. It was encouraging and inspiring and for sure kept us motivated every time someone would send a text that they had signed a new contract.

Who is *not* an effective accountability partner? Your spouse or partner, some family, and some friends. They might let you slide or they might cause resentment. It worked out for my brother and me, but I couldn't be in a group with every member of my family. My husband and I would not be proper accountability for each other because for some issues, our first instinct is to feel attacked or that we have failed if we are questioned.

If you have been struggling with something, there is a coach for it. If you want to reach the next level, a coach can help you do that. I don't think anyone is above a coach. The people who hire Tony Robbins, for example, don't have a problem with motivation. They are already excellent in their fields, but they see the potential to go even farther.

Shameless self-promotion alert: If you need help with your productivity (e.g., email, task, time management), health behaviors (e.g., nutrition, movement, sleep, stress management), or boundaries, complete an application and apply for a complimentary Discovery Session at **www.marceyrader. com**. I'd love to tailor this behavior-change journey to your specific needs. If you are interested in a group experience to master the habits in the book, complete an application at www.workwellplaymore.com/masterclass.

> *I will investigate an accountability group or coach for something I have been struggling with or a goal I want to achieve.*

MONTH TWELVE

PRODUCTIVITY:
Protect Yourself and Others

Privacy: The state or condition of being free from being observed or disturbed by other people.

The state of being free from public attention.

The concept of personal privacy has become looser and less respected in the last decade or two. People can secretly record us and upload it to social media. Our texts and emails can be forwarded without our knowledge. People have even gone so far as to record the aftermath of a traffic accident and post videos of dead people before their families were even notified or ambulances had arrived on the scene (disgusting). The younger a person is, the looser they tend to be with their privacy boundaries. They are used to posting their whereabouts, feelings, observations, and photos on social media without considering down the road ramifications. Another benefit to being in the moment during vacations, concerts, or work trips, and not posting to social media until after you are home is that people don't know that your house is empty and waiting for them to burgle it!

We are also at risk of having our identities stolen. My husband and I have had our credit card information stolen three times, but thankfully, have gotten it straightened out and not been charged. We did lose money in terms of the cost of time spent with the police, speaking to credit agencies, and dealing with the companies that allowed the theft to happen. Even though this chapter ends the book, it may be the most important one. Protecting yourself is also about protecting your family, possibly your business, and anyone with whom you have communicated within the platform that has been compromised. So, yeah, this one is huge.

Novice: Password Manager

Remembering a million passwords is difficult and using the same password over and over is dangerous. A password management program will save time and brainpower. Password programs like **Dashlane** offer free and premium features (You can use this affiliate link: **https://www.dashlane.com/en/cs/3baca9e9** to get 6 months of Dashlane premium for free). They will remember your passwords, alert you when they aren't strong enough, and generate strong passwords for you. They also allow secure storage of credit cards, so that information is available automatically when you purchase online. They have a sharing feature that will enable you to send a username and password to someone else via email that expires after a certain amount of time too. This is great, for instance, when I want my VA to have access to a website temporarily. You can also share via limited access, where people can log in under your username and password, but they don't have access to everything and can't change your password without your knowledge. Bonus: it works across platforms so you can use it on phones, tablets, and computers. I use Dashlane, but there are several other password managers out there.

A feature that will help your loved ones is what I call the "death setting." If something were to happen to me, I have designated two people to have access to all my usernames and passwords. They simply contact Dashlane, and if I don't respond to Dashlane's request after a specified amount of time, my people gain limited or full rights access. A service like this is crucial because if something were to happen to you, someone needs to be able to log in and deactivate or pause your accounts so that you aren't being charged or even worse, that your social media profile is still up two years after your death. Twice I've had people pop up on LinkedIn as people I might want to connect with when those people had died. It's very disconcerting.

> *So many times, people imagine one specific scenario happening in their lives, but so often, something from left field is actually the incident that ends up occurring—and they don't have a plan for that. Taking a 360-degree view to make sure that everyone will have the information they need when they need it is incredibly powerful. It's ultimately the best way to tell the people that you care about that you love them. Nothing makes the grief any easier—but some things can make it so much worse!* —**Annette Adamska, Founder, Back Up Your Life**

Annette Adamska has a company called Back Up Your Life and helps people get their digital lives organized. There's even an online program to walk you through the steps. If it seems daunting, outsource and have Annette coach you through it. The time upfront is worth the peace of mind later.

If you are worried about whether keeping all your passwords in password software is safe, note that security experts recommend password protectors over the passwords that people typically use, which can easily be hacked. Typing in a name using a "3" for an "E" and an "!" for a "1" isn't all that hard to figure out. Password management companies are in the business of protecting your information. They are throwing more resources at doing that than you are with your sticky notes and non-password-protected spreadsheet!

> *Hackers look for low hanging fruit. You just need to be hard enough that they'd rather hack someone else than have to deal with the safeguards you have put in. Other bonuses? Use the sharing features to never have to tell a family member or loved one what the Netflix password is—they can find it themselves!*
> *— Annette Adamska, Founder, Back Up Your Life*

Password management programs also work for businesses. I use Dashlane to give temporary access to freelancers as well as revoke access when someone is done with a project. This saves me from having to email or text passwords, which is one of the worst things you can do with your passwords. If I'm temporarily out of commission, my husband, assistant, or anyone else I have delegated can use the password manager to get access to what they need, while still keeping me safe from hackers.

> *I will stop using a spreadsheet or stickies to keep track of my passwords. I will use a password manager to increase my security online.*

Pro: *Digital Afterlife*

Twenty years ago, the idea of a digital afterlife was not something we had to worry about or something that even existed in our vocabularies, but the Internet has changed everything. You'll be gone so digital afterlife may not matter to you, but it will to family and friends, and maybe your business assets. Just as a Will is for beneficiaries, there are digital afterlife services to help your loved ones clean up your online presence and save them from the heartache and headache of figuring out what to do.

What could your digital afterlife include? Social media accounts, PayPal, eBay, Venmo, online banking, online subscriptions, Amazon accounts—the list goes on and on. You may be signed up for a recurring subscription that takes $150 out of your account every year, and your partner may not realize it until it comes out of the bank account or the fee shows up on the credit card statement. The company may be able to reverse the charge, but do you want your family member to have to call and request it?

I have a special note in Evernote for my husband and my brother (in case something happens to my husband as well) about who to contact, what programs I am subscribed to, and what accounts need to be deactivated. I want to make this extremely easy with as little stress as possible. I consider them my Digital Executors. It also includes instructions for how to see where my contracts stand, if money is owed back to people, and what was in my pipeline.

I would contact an expert to help in the preparation of your digital afterlife as there are state laws that actually prohibit you from using your loved one's accounts after they have passed if there is nothing in writing giving you permission.

> As our work and lives are increasingly carried out online, we must also consider how we can secure our digital accounts and assets in the event of death or incapacity. You can read entire books on this subject. (I know. I wrote one of them.) The simplest advice, however, is to have a plan. Look into Google's Inactive Account Manager and Facebook's Legacy Contacts feature to provide access to the data stored in those accounts. Finally, I also encourage you to speak with your estate attorney to ensure you add powers to your estate planning documents to ensure your executor will be able to carry out your wishes.
> — *Evan Carroll, Author of* Your Digital Afterlife, When Facebook, Flickr, and Twitter are your estate, what's your legacy?

I will make preparations for my digital afterlife and assign two digital executors should something happen to me.

Master: *Wills, Trusts, and Directives*

Most people want to think about anything other than creating a Will or Advanced Health Care Directive. Maybe it's too scary to think about not being around or maybe you think since you don't have a lot of money, it doesn't matter. Well, nothing could be further from the truth. A Will is not for *you* and refusing or procrastinating on creating one is selfish. Yep, I said it. It's downright selfish to force your family to figure out what has to be done after you're gone. And if you think your lack of riches means it will be easy to disseminate your stuff or what's left in your account, know that if you don't state your wishes, your estate will end up in probate for up to a year and the state will determine who gets what, after they take out a large percentage for themselves. Is that where you want your money to end up? And your kids? The courts will decide who they stay with until it's worked out in the system. This is the one thing I am not going to be kind or soft about. Take ownership.

You can quickly and easily set something up via an online service, but I highly recommend consulting an attorney. When I went through the process, I discovered there were a few things that would have been done incorrectly for us and would have cost our families more money to settle. Rules vary state-to-state and an attorney can help you walk through the best option for your situation.

You also need a Health Care Power of Attorney to help make decisions if you are incapacitated. Choose someone you trust who will care about your wishes and who will have the emotional stability to be able to carry out your requests. A Living Will or an Advanced Directive will explicitly state if you want to be kept alive using artificial means or if you have signed a Do Not Resuscitate Order. You also will want to spell out whether you want to donate your tissue or organs and whether you want your body to be cremated, buried, or donated to science. Spell out everything ahead of time, so your family doesn't have to take on this burden during what will be a high-crisis and extremely emotional situation for them.

> *I will create a Will, Health Care Directive, and designate a Health Care Power of Attorney so that my family does not bear an extra burden if something were to happen to me.*

DECLUTTER: Brain

We are inundated with information from TV, podcasts, blog posts, social media feeds, news feeds, radio, and notifications. Infobesity or information overload, information anxiety, or information explosion can actually hinder us from making effective decisions because we are paralyzed by the sheer mass of it all and are afraid of making the "wrong" choice.

As a recovering over-achiever, I felt like I had to stay caught up on all the latest and most popular podcasts, Netflix series, blog posts, thought leaders' ideas, and news events. But I can't. And neither can you.

You are not going to know everything.

Yes! It's true! You can't possibly know everything and at some point, you need that white space in your brain—that emptiness of zero input coming in through your ears or eyes—to allow yourself to actually think about the information you already have. It's this space that allows us to be creative and come up with new ideas.

Novice: Information Vacation

I take *Information Vacations* for one week each quarter. I started this because, as an entrepreneur, I had a lot to learn about areas I wasn't familiar with, like marketing and web design. I was continually reading reference and business books or listening to podcasts to improve my skillset. Even though I enjoy reading and listening to learn, I know sometimes I need to just chill out and read fiction and listen to music. I also have friends with businesses who spend more time learning about their industry than they spend working on their business. It's a great form of procrastination that doesn't always result in revenue. Some days, you just have to put the books down and ready, aim, fire, and learn through experience.

One thing that helped me was to greatly reduce what I'm subscribed to so that I don't see those badges showing me how far behind I am in my reading and listening. I continually question whether a podcast, newsletter, or other information source is of high value for me.

I typically schedule my Information Vacations when I'm on vacation or during the December holidays. I don't learn anything! I just watch fun movies, listen to music, and read fiction. I focus on what I already know and think about how to put it into practice. It gives my brain a break and reduces a lot of screen time. It's not as strict as a digital detox because I'm still working if it's not during a vacation. I'm just not focused on research. This may not be an issue for you, especially if you are cruising in your career and aren't a big reader. For those high achievers out there, give your brain a break every once in a while and soak up the awesomeness of who you already are and what you already know.

> *I will take a minimum of one weekend on*
> _____ *(date) for an Information*
> *Vacation and take a mental fast from media*
> *input into my brain.*

Pro: Digital Communication Free Day

How would you feel if you were only able to communicate face-to-face—no texting, phone, instant messages, social media, or email? If you're under thirty, you might find this to be an incredible challenge. If you're over forty, you may remember this as being our old normal. If we went to a concert, we actually paid attention to what was in front of us instead of taking selfies and live-texting what we were seeing to our friends. I often leave my phone at home if I'm going out with my husband because if I'm with him, I know I won't need to be contacted with any kind of urgency. If you have kids, you may need to do something different. My friend Sylvia asks the babysitter to text her when the kids are asleep so she can relax and not feel that she has to check her phone for a message.

But really, when was the last time you were completely present with yourself or the person you were with for an entire day? Start small by only checking your phone a few times during the day for a limited time. Or you could take this one step further and be screen-free for 24 hours. Turn off your Wi-Fi. Shut your phone completely off and put it somewhere inconvenient. Truly focus on whatever you are doing in the moment and the people you are with.

> *I will take an entire day to myself or the people I am with, screen-free.*

Master: *Weekend Digital Detox*

Digital detoxes where people check into retreat centers, hotels, resorts, or campgrounds and turn in their phones are becoming more popular because without being forced to do it, many people can't. I have clients who used to take cruises on purpose because there was no Wi-Fi, and they could relax. Now they complain because cruises have Internet access and are no longer their "safe place." Campgrounds and wilderness areas even have cellular access these days, which is excellent in case of emergency but not great if you are addicted to your phone. Once when I was in the Grand Canyon, I was admiring the beauty of the vast expanse of the canyon and a guy next to me was surprised when his phone rang. He took the call and I heard him say, "Uh . . . we are hiking in the Grand Canyon on vacation, can I call you back?" What surprised me was that he even answered the phone.

I think digital detox is especially important when you are on vacation because I often feel like people are more concerned about posting their experiences than having the experiences! They can't even wait until they are back at the hotel. (And really, why does it have to be in real time?) They use the moment of experience to post a photo. If the extraordinary number of people who have died trying to get the most amazing selfies (i.e., hanging off of the edge of El Capitan in Yosemite) doesn't make you rethink how much we live our lives on our devices, I don't know what will. There is no need to feel validated through someone's like or comment, especially when you are on vacation. Enjoy your moment and the people you are with.

As a business owner, I have my assistant be the only gate-keeper for me to receive calls or messages. If it's truly urgent, she will contact me, but really, I'm not performing emergency surgery, so urgency is rarely an issue. I don't recommend this, but you are an adult (perhaps controlled by a small electronic device!)—so, if you feel like you really need to check your email or voice mail, set time frames, like on Monday, Thursday, and Friday of your vacation or in the morning and evening for a maximum of ten minutes. Ask someone to hold you accountable.

I also have a rule that my family is not to call me if something bad has happened while I am on vacation. If I can't do anything about it, all it does is ruin my vacation. I managed an employee once who had a family member admitted to the hospital. She was unable to get a flight until the next afternoon and couldn't do anything to help anyway, but for 36 hours she was a wreck, all by herself, in a hotel room.

Even more challenging, I've seen a woman on a business trip get an upsetting call that put her into such a frantic state TSA wouldn't allow her to board, which put her into even more hysterics, and they had to escort her away. I can't imagine how horrible it must have been for her.

We need to save ourselves from ourselves, so if you know the FOMO or curiosity will be too much, give your phone to someone else or go somewhere that has no cellular service. You don't have to stay captive to your device!

> *I will schedule one weekend (or week!) as a digital detox. I will save myself from myself (if necessary) by giving my phone to someone else or going somewhere remote with no cellular access.*

HEALTH: Future Planning

If you own a business or work in any kind of sales role, you make projections or have targets that you want to hit. If you sign up for a race, you typically have goals for reaching the finish line. I'm a natural goal-setter and spent the first five years of my business focusing so much on the why, how, and numbers that I realized that I could take that same energy and focus on my personal life to achieve success in the business that means more than anything—me and my husband!

Novice: 90-Day Vision

If you want to test this one on yourself first or if you are single, start your 90-Day Vision just for you. I adapted this from a 90-Day Vision template used in the Savor the Success mastermind, which is no longer functioning but was an integral part of my business life at the time. Each quarter sit down in a special cafe, outside, or somewhere that makes you feel relaxed and inspired and write down your vision for the next 90 days.

A sample template with examples is below. List no more than three goals in any area so that you can prioritize. Remember, our brains remember things in three's more easily, and any more than three goals is too much to focus on.

- **In 90 days:**

  General:
  I want to feel relaxed at our family vacation.
  I want to have reduced anxiety when flying.

  Health goals:
  I will complete the anxiety meditation series.
  I will be able to complete 15 pull-ups in a row.

  Business goals:
  I will nail my Key5 conference workshop.
  I will hit my $$$ revenue goal.
  I will complete writing six book chapters.

  Personal growth goals:
  I will read or listen to eight full-length books.

  Wouldn't it be amazing if: (*This isn't a goal, it's something that would be amazing that* **might happen.**) *If it happens every quarter, you probably aren't making it amazing enough!)*
  I was asked to keynote at the Big Boom international conference.
  I had another waitlist for clients.
  I could send my husband to the national woodturning conference.

You can do just one thing or a few. Add whatever you want. It's just a template. Visit it every week as a reminder of your Vision.

> *I will create a 90-Day Vision for myself.*

Pro: *90-Day Family or Friend Vision*

The next step would be to create a 90-Day Vision for your family. I was a little nervous when I approached my husband about doing this with me, but it has become one of our favorite times together, and we look forward to reviewing it every week. On Sundays after breakfast, over coffee, we go through our visions. It keeps things top of mind for us. We also use this time to do a review of our calendars, finances, and house projects. I've had some clients do this with their kids as well. One of them said his eight-year-old son's "amazing" vision idea was that his dad would have lunch with him at school one day. He had never expressed that he wanted this to happen. It was a simple thing for his dad to do and has resulted in a once-a-month tradition for them.

Sample template:

- In 90 days, Marcey feels:
- In 90 days, Kevin feels:
- Personal goals:
- Family goals:
- Money goals:
- House goals: (We live in a fixer-upper, so this helps us plan what we want to tackle that quarter.)
- Business/Career goals:
- Special dates/events:
- Kevin was awesome when he . . . (I say something that Kevin did that week that I really liked or that was particularly awesome!)

- Marcey was awesome when she . . . (Kevin says the same about me.)
- Wouldn't it be amazing if we:

Try it with your family. If you're single, you can do this with a friend for accountability or support. I've had one workshop attendee do this with his kids in college. They join in once a month via video.

> **I will expand the 90-Day Vision to my family or a friend.**

Master: *Abundance*

Have you ever sat down and written a list of what makes you feel abundant? The concept of having an abundance mentality was coined by Steven Covey and is defined as a fundamental business concept in which a person believes there are enough resources and success to share with others. "Abundant life," according to Wikipedia, "is the fullness of joy and strength for the mind, body, and soul." My business coach, **Shauna Van Bogart**, once had me list all of the things that make me feel abundant and also make me happy, confident, and deserving of earning everything that I have. I have continued to expand on the list, and it now covers two pages. My friend Wendy uses the term "chi-chi." Whatever makes you feel "kick-ass," use that terminology.

When I was growing up, I saw my mom and the other women in my family become a product of the burnt toast. You know what I mean—if one piece of toast gets burned, they eat that piece. My mom sacrificed and bought everything for us but never focused on herself. I see many parents, but especially moms, whether they work outside the home or not, put their needs last in similar ways. I find myself doing this with my husband.

Doing or having things that make me feel abundant is essential to me. When I focus on what makes me feel abundant, I am showing myself respect, care, and that I'm worth it. When I shared this list with my husband, some of the things surprised him and just like the eight-year-old sharing his "amazing" with his dad, it made my husband aware of what makes me feel happy. Some things are so simple, he makes sure that they happen.

Five things that make me feel abundant:

- Drinking a cappuccino out of *a real mug* at a cafe, because drinking a fancy beverage out of paper is a misdemeanor

- Having my car cleaned inside and out

- Airline club access

- Sitting on my screened-in porch listening to the rain

- Wait staff knowing my name and what I like before I order

> *Write down at least three things that make you feel abundant and share the list with someone.*

WHAT'S NEXT?

You did it! Congratulations on making it through 12 months of behavior change! High Fives and Fist Bumps! There are so many directions you can take at this point. If you completed the Novice steps, start over and hit the Pro. If you skipped around, go back and hit the ones you missed. If there are a few that are still challenging for you, focus on those for the next round.

If you have been less than consistent about your habit changes, don't beat yourself up. Behavior change is going to involve setbacks. When you learned to ride a bike, you probably didn't sit down, start pedaling, and then sign up for the Tour de France. You fell off, skinned your knees, and then got up and started again, except this time, you were a little ahead. Each time you fell, you learned something. You knew a little better how to brake, or shift, or keep your balance. It's the same with behavior change. Every time you start again, you'll be starting from a place of knowing more than you did before.

I didn't stop after completing my list of 100 habits. As my life changes, my business develops, my health shifts, and my relationships change, I have to reevaluate and adjust. What works for you now may not work for you later or what you couldn't do before, you can do now because you have a new job, you are in a new relationship (or newly single), or you decided to down- or up-size your home. That's the beauty of this book. You can take whatever you want and need at the time and incorporate it in a way that makes sense. Then you can revisit these habit changes again and again.

Don't forget you also receive the *exclusive bonus* I created to add to your tool belt. A hidden online bonus chapter can be accessed with links to all the references, companies, software programs, books, and other resources I have mentioned. You'll get videos, webinars, and downloads to help you further develop your new behavior changes.

Visit **https://www.workwellplaymore.com/books/ wwpm-bonus-sign-up/** and enter your name and email address. You'll receive the password via email to access the page.

If you need more help via self-paced video training, head over to **www.workwellplaymorecourse.com** and check out the *Work Well. Play More! Health and Productivity* online course where you can learn over 300 behavioral shifts. Use the code *whiteboard* for 25 percent off. There are courses for *Email Extinguisher, Conquer the Calendar, Task Mastery,* and *Energy Escalators* that will help you put all of the suggestions into practice.

For group coaching specifically on the behaviors in this book, visit **www.workwellplaymore.com/masterclass** and sign up for our online group coaching program. Having a supplemental accountability experience with video Q&A sessions and hearing the strategies of other people going through the program can greatly increase the odds that you'll succeed. Plus, you'll meet new people with their own challenges and strategies, and it's more fun!

Need a high-touch personal strategy with accountability and support? Reach out to me at **www.marceyrader.com** and complete an application for coaching to see if we are a good fit for each other. If you are part of a team, company, or association that would like speaking or workshops centered around productivity and health behaviors, visit **www.workwellplaymore. com**.

Interested in buying the book in bulk or for your book club? I give discounts for ten or more print copies. Please email books@workwellplaymore.com for an estimate.

I hope you can look back and see the accomplishments you've made, the successes you've had, and the mental and emotional mountain you climbed. Here's to you . . .

High Fives and Fist Bumps!
Marcey

SPECIAL REQUEST

I sincerely thank you for reading my book. Whether you bought it, received it as a gift, or borrowed it, you made it this far so it must have meant something. If you feel like this book was valuable, whether you freakin' loved it or just kind of liked it, please leave a review on Amazon and Goodreads.

Without sounding like someone desperately needing a friend, in today's world where anyone can write and self-publish, reviews are one of the primary ways other readers find books like this one, especially in the giant categories of organization, health, and productivity. The average digital-only self-published book sells only 250 copies in its lifetime. Did you know only one percent of people who read a book will review it? After I became an author and realized how much it meant, I started reviewing every book I read. *Please be my One Percent* on Amazon and Goodreads. You don't need to write a whole story, just jot down a couple of things you valued from the book.

Writing and self-publishing are both challenging and rewarding experiences. I'm able to continue doing this with the help of people who buy my book. While every author knows the importance of reviews, the reader doesn't always get the impact. Please know that every review is read and helps my book move up in the ranks to be more searchable. It also affords people who are struggling with challenges that this book addresses find help. Taking a few minutes out of your already time-pressed schedule to write a review on Amazon. com or Goodreads will make my day and let others know this book exists. I promise to send good vibes your way.

BONUS!

Now that you have your copy of *Work Well. Play More! Productive, Clutter-free, Healthy Living – One Step at a Time*, you're on your way to achieving behavior change you didn't believe possible. You also have access to the *exclusive bonus* I created to add to your tool belt. In this hidden online bonus chapter, you will find links to all the references, companies, software, programs, and books I mention here. You'll also find videos, webinars, and downloads to help you stay focused and further develop your new behavior changes.

All you have to do to get this exclusive bonus is visit **https://www.workwellplaymore.com/books/wwpm-bonus-sign-up/** and enter your email address. You'll receive the password via email to access the page.

Need even more help? Check out my Work Well. Play More! Health and Productivity online course at **www.workwellplaymorecourse.com**. Use the code *whiteboard* to receive a 25 percent discount. There are also mini courses for specific challenges such as *Email Extinguisher, Conquer the Calendar, Task Mastery,* and *Energy Escalators* that will help you put all of these suggestions into practice.

Recommended Books

The Power of Less, by Leo Babauta

Unclutter Your Life in One Week - Erin Doland

The Power of Habit - Charles Duhigg

Deep Work - Cal Newport

Better Than Before - Gretchen Rubin

ACKNOWLEDGMENTS

I would like to High Five and Fist Bump the following people *in no particular order:*

My husband Kevin—for being patient with my behavior changes, moving not once but twice to down-size our home, and for deciding to go all in and adopt some of the behaviors as well!

My 500 Club mastermind—Stan Phelps, David Rendall, Justin Jones-Fosu, Jeff Nischwitz, and Kevin Snyder—who help me see what's possible, provide invaluable feedback, and let me pick the food for our meetings.

My business coach, Shauna Van Bogart—who expands my mind and keeps me from feeling small (and wearing ruffles).

Wendy Gates Corbett—for going to Mexico with me four years in a row to find our inner chi-chi.

Business coach Vania Clark Butler—who first put me on the path of seeing what I do as a true business.

My Vistage Executive Chair, Janet Boudreau—for being one of my biggest cheerleaders and recognizing the value I bring to the table.

My Vistage group and Vistage International—the feedback, insights, and knowledge I gain from being part of this organization are worth every penny I pay and more. It is a mastermind in business every time I speak and attend.

Lilly Ferrick, my Mexican sister from another mister, and Todd Rader, my brother and fastest meme-finder known to man—for pushing me to hit the $$$ goals, and keeping me motivated with group text-a-thons and Habanero Chocolate Lattes.

Stephanie Scotti—for feedback, support, funny hats, and pecans.

Mary-Lynn Fulton, for bringing me in to Vertex Pharmaceuticals, supporting my new business and seeing that I can do a complete pivot in my career and be successful.

The PRiSM speaker mastermind led by Stan Phelps—without a doubt, I would not be where I am today as a speaker without this fantastic group of people sharing their wisdom.

My kick-ass clients, both private and corporate—who inspire me every day to be better.

Super Summer Busto—for being my first client and introducing me to Sweet 100 tomatoes and Summer Burpees.

My stylist and friend Michelle Scaraglino—for giving me

back my decisions, preventing me from wasting time in my closet, for monthly dinners, and for making my Hazelnut Torte birthday cake four years in a row.

My financial planner Bob Williams, my accountant Joel Levy, and my financial coach Sylvia Inks—for keeping me on the path to financial abundance and supporting my goal of debt free at age forty five. (Woot Woot!)

My House Assistant Karin—for folding my clothes better than the Gap, chopping my vegetables so I don't end up in the emergency room (again), and for seeing what needs done and doing it.

My beta readers Jessica Coscia, Lisa Wood, Sara Shelp, Sylvia Inks, Eric Syfrett, Mary-Lynn Fulton, and Michael Clegg— for giving me the feedback to know this is a book to be proud of.

Emily Crookston, my developmental editor, for keeping my voice and not letting me give in to opinions that weren't mine.

Lee Heinrich, my editor, for forgiving my grammatical errors and my inability to use quotations correctly in a sentence.

Mr. Coffee Coffee Warmer—for keeping my coffee and tea warm every day and for being one of the best $10 gifts a person could buy.

My parents—if I didn't grow up with some of these habits, I would most definitely not have a book to write. For all the embarrassment, you get royalties.

About the Author

Marcey Rader wears many shoes (like hats, but more active): accomplished corporate ladder-climber, business owner, kombucha brewer, and Skip-Bo player. She's the founder of **Marcey Rader Coaching** and the **Work Well. Play More! Institute** where entrepreneurs, business leaders, and their entire teams seek out new life and peak productivity through private and team coaching to reach their potential and leave business burnout in the dust.

She's an award-winning, top-rated speaker who packs presentations with actionable advice and real-world wisdom. Her speaking roster is alive with keynotes and workshops for Fortune 100 companies, startups, and everyone in between from North Dakota to Dubai in industries ranging from steel manufacturing to biotech.

She's the author of two previous books—Amazon best-seller *Beyond Travel: A Road Warrior's Survival Guide* and *Hack the Mobile Lifestyle: 6 Steps to Work Well and Play More!*—and creator of a **digital course**. She's also a regular guest on and contributor to a whole bunch of media outlets.

Marcey lives with her husband, Kevin, a professional percussionist and teacher, in Raleigh, North Carolina, and can be found searching out movement opportunities, drinking iced coffee (without sugar!), and hoop dancing blind-folded in her backyard.

Made in the USA
Middletown, DE
29 November 2019